Table of Contents

Preface... xi

1. Introduction... 1
   What Are Web Components?   2
      HTML Templates   3
      HTML Imports   3
      Custom Elements   4
      The Shadow DOM   4
   Why Web Components?   4

Part I.   UI Core Concepts

2. Creating a Solid Foundation................................. 11
   The Importance of a DOM Abstraction Layer   11
   API Design and Widget Life Cycle   12
   The Inheritance Pattern   14
   Dependencies   15
   Optimization   16
   A Web Component Is Not JavaScript Alone   17
   Example Widget   18
      The Voltron Widget Base Class   18
      Dialog Class   20
      Dialog CSS and HTML   21
   Summary   22

3. Normal Flow and Positioning................................. 23
   Normal Flow   23

Positioning Elements   24
    offsetParent   25
    Positioning   26
Calculating an Element's Position   29
    Relative to the Viewport   29
    Relative to the Document   30
Positioning the Dialog Widget   31
Summary   31

4. Understanding and Managing z-index. **33**
What Exactly Is the z-index Property?   33
Rendering Layers, Stacking Order, and z-index   34
    Default Stacking Orders   34
    Overriding the Default Stacking Order   35
Stacking Contexts   36
    How Is a Stacking Context Created?   36
    Increasing Complexity   37
Managing z-indexes   37
    z-index Manager   38
Converting to a jQuery Plugin   45
Adding z-index Management to the Dialog Widget   47
Summary   47

Part II.   Building Our UI

5. Cloning Nodes. **51**
Using the cloneNode Method   52
Using jQuery.clone   53
Continuation of the Dialog Widget   55
Summary   55

6. Constructing an Overlay. **57**
Defining an API   57
Utilities   59
    Detecting Scrollbar Width   59
    Accounting for the Scrollbar When Calculating a Containing Element's
        Width   60
    Getting an Element's Dimensions and Coordinates   61
    Listening for Resize and Scrolling Events   62
Updating Options   62
Destroying   63

Positioning   63
    Positioning an Element Relative to the Viewport or Another Element   64
    Positioning an Element Relative to Another Element   66
Adding the Overlay to the Dialog Widget   68
Summary   69

7. Making Elements Draggable. 71
Mouse Events   71
    $.mousemove   71
    $.mousedown   72
    $.mouseup   72
Mouse Events Best Practices   72
    1. Bind $.mousemove on $.mousedown   72
    2. Unbind $.mousemove on $.mouseup   73
    3. Bind $.mouseup to the <body>   73
    4. Namespace All Event Bindings   73
Defining an API   74
Creating a Drag Handle   75
Making Things Move   75
    $.mousedown Handler   75
    $.mousemove Handler   76
    $.mouseup Handler   77
Destroying a Draggable Instance   78
Making the Dialog Widget Draggable   78
Summary   79

8. Resizing Elements. 81
Mouse Events and Best Practices (Recap)   81
    Events   81
    Best Practices   82
Resizing an Element   82
Making a Resizable API   83
Defining Drag Handles   84
Binding Event Handlers   85
    $.mousedown Handler   85
    $.mousemove Handler   87
    $.mouseup Handler   87
Destroying a Resizable Instance   88
Completed Resizing Library   88
Making the Dialog Widget Resizable   92
Summary   94

9. Completing the Dialog Widget. **95**
    Styling the Widget   95
        Adding CSS   95
    Concatenating the JavaScript   96
    Summary   97

Part III.   Building HTML5 Web Components

10. Utilizing Templates. **101**
    Understanding the Importance of Templates   102
        Deferring the Processing of Resources   102
        Deferring the Rendering of Content   103
        Hiding the Content from the DOM   103
    Creating and Using a Template   103
        Detecting Browser Support   103
        Placing a Template in Markup   103
        Adding a Template to the DOM   104
    Converting the Dialog Component to a Template   104
        Creating a Wrapper API for the Dialog Template   105
        Instantiating a Dialog Component Instance   106
    Abstracting the Dialog Template Wrapper   106
    Summary   107

11. Working with the Shadow DOM. **109**
    What Is the Shadow DOM?   109
    Shadow DOM Basics   110
        Shadow Host   110
        Shadow Root   110
    Using a Template with the Shadow DOM   111
    Shadow DOM Styling   112
        Style Encapsulation   112
        Styling the Host Element   113
        Styling Shadow Root Elements from the Parent Page   115
    Content Projection   117
        Projection via a Content Tag   117
        Projection via Content Selectors   118
        Getting Distributed Nodes and Insertion Points   119
    Shadow Insertion Points   120
    Events and the Shadow DOM   122
    Updating the Dialog Template to Use the Shadow DOM   122
        Dialog Markup   123

  Dialog API 124
  Updating the Dialog show Method 124
  Instantiating a Dialog Component Instance 125
 Summary 125

12. Creating Custom Elements.. **127**
 Introducing Custom Elements 128
 Registering Custom Elements 128
 Extending Elements 129
  Extending Custom Elements 129
  Extending Native Elements 130
 Defining Properties and Methods 130
 Resolving Custom Elements 131
 Hooking Into Custom Element Life Cycles 131
  createdCallback 132
  attachedCallback 132
  detachedCallback 132
  attributeChangedCallback 133
 Styling Custom Elements 133
 Utilizing Templates and the Shadow DOM with Custom Elements 134
 Converting the Dialog Component to a Custom Element 135
  Creating the Dialog Custom Element 136
  Implementing the Dialog Custom Element's Callbacks 136
  Implementing the Dialog Custom Element API 137
  Showing the Dialog 138
 Summary 138

13. Importing Code.. **139**
 Declaring an Import 139
 Accessing an Import's Content 140
  Referencing Documents 141
  Applying Styles 142
  Accessing Templates 143
  Executing JavaScript 144
 Understanding Imports in Relation to the Main Document 144
  Parsing Imports 144
  Cross-Domain Considerations 145
  Subimports 145
 Loading Custom Elements 145
 Importing the Dialog 146
 Summary 147

Part IV. Testing, Building, and Deploying Components with Polymer

14. Introducing Polymer... **151**

Polymer Elements   154
   Adding Style   156
   External Resources   157
   Filtering Expressions   157
Template Syntax   159
   Data Binding   159
   Block Repetition   159
   Bound Scopes   160
   Conditional Blocks   160
   Multiple Template Directives at Once   161
Attributes and Properties—Your Element's API   161
   Naked Attributes   161
   Published Properties   162
   Instance Methods   162
Polymer's JavaScript APIs   163
   Life Cycle Methods   163
   Events   164
   Managing Delayed Work   164
Summary   165

15. Porting Our Dialog to Polymer... **167**

Why Port Anything to Polymer at All?   168
The Direct Port   169
   Managing Dependencies   169
   Installing Dependencies with Bower   171
   Getting Started   173
That Was Easy—A Little Too Easy!   182
jQuery in a Polymer World   182
   What Does jQuery Provide?   183
   Removing jQuery   183
   The Verdict on jQuery   186
Summary   187

16. Testing Web Components... **189**

PhantomJS 1   190
PhantomJS 2   191
Selenium WebDriver   191
Karma   191

Test Specs   196
Running Our Tests   199
Summary   201

17. Packaging and Publishing... **203**
Vulcanize   204
Gulp   209
Grunt   210
    Gruntfiles   212
    Grunt Tasks   213
    Registering Tasks   214
    Grunt Configuration   214
Publishing with Bower   219
    Registering the Component   220
Summary   221

18. Final Words.. **223**
Where Do We Go from Here?   223
    Polymer   224
    Mozilla X-Tag   224
    document-register-element   225
    WebComponents.org   225
    CustomElements.io   225
Good Luck!   226

Index.. **227**

Preface

Why We Wrote This Book

Web development has not stopped evolving since I stumbled into the field over 13 years ago. If anything, the rate at which it is evolving is increasing. If you take a look at the investment that Google has made in Polymer and web components, it is probably safe to bet that web components will play a large role in web development in the near future as browsers implement more support for them. There are still some issues that need to be addressed, such as search engine optimization (SEO) concerns, but I do not think web components are going away, and I don't think this is bad. The introduction of web components (or a similar standard for extending, packaging, encapsulating, and importing discrete UI components) is long overdue in web development. Even if you do not put all your stock in web components—for example, lifting back the curtain and seeing how the Great Oz accomplishes his UI wizardry, making an element draggable—they can be very useful.

Glenn Vanderburg said, "Developers should always understand one layer of abstraction below their everyday work." I agree with this statement, and I would argue that widget libraries, jQuery plugins, and even jQuery are the levels of abstraction at which most frontend engineers operate on a daily basis. The level just below that consists of the DOM manipulations these libraries perform, and the DOM and its native APIs. Understanding precisely what these libraries are doing will enable you to write more efficient code on a daily basis and prepare you for the great awakening.

Inevitably, there will come a time when one of these libraries does not fit nicely into the use case with which your product manager or information architect has gifted you—at which point, you either sink or swim. I for one would have preferred to have some swimming lessons before my day arrived, but I was not that fortunate.

I was tasked with making a fixed-width portal product fluid-width, and all of the portlets resizable. Sounds easy, right? I was informed that this had been attempted more than once before, and that previous developers had failed and said it was impossible. Well, that was encouraging. On top of this, Internet Explorer 9 had just hit the market, and due to technical debt we were running three different versions of jQuery and two different versions of jQuery UI, none of which worked well with IE9. So, before I could even start the resizing work I had to move to a single version of jQuery and jQuery UI that played nicely with IE9. You might think that moving to a single version of each library would be a simple process, but I quickly realized why we had accumulated the massive technical debt. We were running a myriad of jQuery plugins ranging from bad to awful in quality and old to ancient in web time. In addition to breaking our code, the upgrade broke the majority of these plugins. This required upgrading and patching several plugins, and replacing others. This in turn involved an intimate knowledge of the DOM, which I did not have. I console logged, reverse engineered, and consumed Stack Overflow (*http://stackoverflow.com*) until I had solved every problem. This was all before I could even get started on the column resizing and portlet changes.

Next, I got some ridiculous requirement that the portlet column resizing had to look precisely like a mock that had already been approved. It also had to behave just as the approved specification described. There was not a plugin in existence that would meet these requirements. Marvelous. I got to write my own.

Once I had that spaghetti code written, I had to make all the portlets and every widget resizable. All of these events had to be timed properly, and nothing could spill out of containers while resizing. `setTimeout` and I began a love affair that still continues to this day.

If you can relate to this story, then you likely have your own. If so, like me, you probably hacked something together that was a hodgepodge of Stack Overflow responses and miscellaneous jQuery plugins held together by some glue code you wrote that have 100 different branches to account for all the anomalies that occurred due to your lack of understanding. I have been there, and it is not fun. This experience is why I wrote this book.

In addition to not drowning, there are some other benefits to understanding how the lower-level parts of UI components function:

- It allows you to define an API that makes sense to you—jQuery plugins are not everyone's cup of tea.
- It gives you full control over the entire stack, which makes debugging easier and allows you to decide at what layer a change should occur.
- It allows you to decide which features are important and to limit your footprint in cases where file size is of great concern (e.g., mobile applications).
- It allows you to make optimizations that fit your applications and use cases.

Lastly, I think that it is every frontend engineer's job to understand the DOM and vanilla JavaScript. This understanding, and the ability to design solutions, is what sets frontend engineers apart from frontend developers.

What This Book Is

The primary goal of this book is to provide the foundational knowledge required to develop and deploy web components. It is intended to be an introduction and to inspire, not to be an exhaustive resource on the subject matter. This foundational knowledge has been divided into four parts, preceded by a general introduction to web components and the areas we will tackle in this book. Each of these sections and their chapters will build upon a working code example.

Part I, UI Core Concepts

The first part covers core concepts such as cloning nodes, rendering layers, stacking contexts, and z-index that are necessary for understanding how to properly position, drag, and resize elements. These concepts are often misunderstood or only partially understood, which can lead to poor design decisions and implementations. These poor decisions can have a significant impact on the performance and maintainability of your code. If you already have a firm grasp on these concepts, then feel free to skip ahead to Part II.

The base class component and the dialog component that are used throughout the rest of the book are introduced in Part I. If you skip ahead and later decide that you would like to learn about the design and implementation details, then refer back to Chapter 2.

Part II, Building Our UI

The second part provides an introduction to concepts and patterns that are typically abstracted away from day-to-day frontend development by libraries such as Dojo (*http://dojotoolkit.org*), jQuery UI (*http://jqueryui.com*), Kendo UI (*http://www.kendoui.com*), and Twitter Bootstrap (*http://getbootstrap.com*). These concepts and patterns are used to implement UI components that you probably work with on a daily basis as a front-end engineer. The benefits that these abstractions and UI components provide cannot be understated. I highly recommend leveraging a base library such as jQuery UI that provides good life cycles, extension points, and access to utility functions and helper classes. If you need a more lightweight foundation you can explore using jQuery++ (*http://jquerypp.com*), which provides APIs for dragging, dropping, resizing, etc. in a single 162 KB file. It also allows you to cherry-pick features, further reducing the file size.

A practical application of these concepts and patterns is illustrated by the continuation of the dialog component that was introduced in Part I.

If you are already familiar with these patterns or you would prefer to dive right into the meat of web components, then start with Part III.

Part III, Building HTML5 Web Components

The third section provides an introduction to web components as defined by the World Wide Web Consortium (W3C) and implemented by browsers. This section takes the working example built in and and converts it into a fully functioning web component.

Part IV, Testing, Building, and Deploying Components with Polymer

The fourth section covers how Google's Polymer (*http://www.polymer-project.org*) bridges the web component implementation gaps in today's browsers and provides convenient APIs for creating extendable web components. It then guides you through converting your web component from Part III into a Polymer component. Finally, it shows how to package and deploy the raw web component and the Polymerized version using different package managers.

What This Book Isn't

The intent of this book is not to be the definitive guide for developing web components across the entire spectrum of devices used to access the Internet. That would be an impossible endeavor, for two key reasons.

First, the capabilities of the browser have increased significantly in recent years, and the Internet has transformed from a document delivery mechanism into a quasi application platform. This transformation has made the browser a much more robust and feature-rich platform than I ever imagined possible back when I was using tables to lay out pages and testing them in Netscape 4. There are now many new techniques for achieving what would have been spectacular feats of JavaScript pixel pushing using CSS alone. These native features continuously evolve, but are adopted at differing rates by browser vendors. Implementation varies across browsers as well, because browser vendors base their implementations on their own interpretations of the W3C specifications. These features are very relevant to web component development, but this brave new browser world is a book topic in its own right. Inclusion of this level of detail is out of scope. While it is very relevant, it is not required for web component development.

Secondly, the number of device types and vendors—smartphones, tablets, phablets, etc.—has increased significantly over the past five years. This proliferation of new devices and manufacturers has reintroduced limitations that we assumed were issues of the past: limited processing power, limited memory, smaller form factors, poor network connectivity, etc. This influx of new devices has impacted web development in interesting ways, and introduced new concepts such as responsive design and adaptive design. They have also introduced new interaction patterns, such as the touch event and gestures. All the devices have their own sets of quirks. The new and expanding mobile market is a field of its own within the web development world, though, and too deep a topic to include here.

Trying to account for these complexities and others in web development when authoring a book of this nature is simply not feasible. The book would be larger than *The Art of Computer Programming* and out of date before the first chapter was complete.

In addition to issues relating to the number of devices on the market and varying device capabilities, it is equally import to note that the W3C Web Components specification is a working specification. As a result, information contained in this book will likely become dated and require the publication of new editions as the specification is finalized. A best effort will be made to follow the specification as closely as possible.

Conventions Used in This Book

The following typographical conventions are used in this book:

Italic
Indicates new terms, URLs, email addresses, filenames, and file extensions.

`Constant width`
Used for program listings, as well as within paragraphs to refer to program elements such as variable or function names, databases, data types, environment variables, statements, and keywords.

`Constant width bold`
Shows commands or other text that should be typed literally by the user.

`Constant width italic`
Shows text that should be replaced with user-supplied values or by values determined by context.

This icon signifies a tip or suggestion.

This icon signifies a general note.

 This icon indicates a warning or caution.

Using Code Examples

Supplemental material (code examples, exercises, etc.) is available for download at *https://github.com/webcomponentsbook*.

This book is here to help you get your job done. In general, if example code is offered with this book, you may use it in your programs and documentation. You do not need to contact us for permission unless you're reproducing a significant portion of the code. For example, writing a program that uses several chunks of code from this book does not require permission. Selling or distributing a CD-ROM of examples from O'Reilly books does require permission. Answering a question by citing this book and quoting example code does not require permission. Incorporating a significant amount of example code from this book into your product's documentation does require permission.

We appreciate, but do not require, attribution. An attribution usually includes the title, author, publisher, and ISBN. For example: "*Developing Web Components* by Jarrod Overson and Jason Strimpel (O'Reilly). Copyright 2015 Jarrod Overson and Jason Strimpel, 978-1-491-94902-3."

If you feel your use of code examples falls outside fair use or the permission given above, feel free to contact us at *permissions@oreilly.com*.

Safari® Books Online

 *Safari Books Online* is an on-demand digital library that delivers expert content in both book and video form from the world's leading authors in technology and business.

Technology professionals, software developers, web designers, and business and creative professionals use Safari Books Online as their primary resource for research, problem solving, learning, and certification training.

Safari Books Online offers a range of plans and pricing for enterprise, government, education, and individuals.

Members have access to thousands of books, training videos, and prepublication manuscripts in one fully searchable database from publishers like O'Reilly Media, Prentice Hall Professional, Addison-Wesley Professional, Microsoft Press, Sams, Que, Peachpit Press, Focal Press, Cisco Press, John Wiley & Sons, Syngress, Morgan Kaufmann, IBM Redbooks, Packt, Adobe Press, FT Press, Apress, Manning, New Riders, McGraw-Hill, Jones & Bartlett, Course Technology, and hundreds more. For more information about Safari Books Online, please visit us online.

How to Contact Us

Please address comments and questions concerning this book to the publisher:

O'Reilly Media, Inc.
1005 Gravenstein Highway North
Sebastopol, CA 95472
800-998-9938 (in the United States or Canada)
707-829-0515 (international or local)
707-829-0104 (fax)

We have a web page for this book, where we list errata, examples, and any additional information. You can access this page at *http://bit.ly/developing-web-components*.

To comment or ask technical questions about this book, send email to *bookquestions@oreilly.com*.

For more information about our books, courses, conferences, and news, see our website at *http://www.oreilly.com*.

Find us on Facebook: *http://facebook.com/oreilly*

Follow us on Twitter: *http://twitter.com/oreillymedia*

Watch us on YouTube: *http://www.youtube.com/oreillymedia*

Acknowledgments

Jason Strimpel

First, I would like to thank my wife Lasca for her encouragement and understanding. I cannot imagine a better partner in life. I have never known a more intelligent, beautiful, and unique person. I love you. You are my favorite everything. Beep boop.

I would also like to thank my manager, Claude Jones, for his guidance and help. Without it, this book would not exist.

I would like to thank my coauthor Jarrod Overson for agreeing to step in and write Part IV. If you sometimes think you're faking it, then I am doomed, as you are definitely a more gifted writer, speaker, and engineer than me.

Many thanks to Simon St.Laurent for hearing out my half-baked idea, and providing the feedback that shaped it into an acceptable book proposal. Also, my editor Brian Anderson is the most patient person I have ever known. Without him this book would be nothing more than the inner workings of my mind without context and would not be understood by anyone expect myself. Thank you Brian.

Finally, I would like to thank all the silent partners—the engineers who write much better code than I ever will and have taught me innumerable lessons. They choose to remain out of the public eye, but if you are lucky enough run across one of them in your career—trust me, you will know it— then listen to them. It is because of these silent partners that I am even passable at best for an engineer and that I am able to share what little knowledge I do posses.

Jarrod Overson

None of my work would have been possible without the support and patience of my wife, Kate Lane. For years now she has accommodated my ramblings about JavaScript, particles, and physics simulations while always being supportive and motivating. Thank you for giving me the opportunities to speak abroad, code into the night, and spend far too much time organizing community events. Without your support none of what I have now would have been possible, including my two beautiful children.

Thank you Finn, for bringing so much joy into my life. All of your great ideas leave me amazed and thrilled to be your father. Thank you Norah, for always being able to put a smile on my face. Both of you have been my motivation to be a father and person that you can be proud of.

Finally, thank you, Jason, for thinking of me when putting this book together. You're one of San Diego's best developers and it's always an honor working with you. I hope to be able to work with you many more times in the future.

CHAPTER 1

Introduction

Jarrod Overson and Jason Strimpel

Oh, good, you're here! Welcome! We hope you're in for a fun ride. If you're the type of person who skips the prefaces of books, we need to go over something real quick: this book is set up in a way that takes you through basic widget creation from a jQuery background and then translates that knowledge and understanding first into the world of web components, and then into that of Polymerized web components (web components created using the Polymer framework).

Web components are on the bleeding edge, barely supported in the most modern of modern browsers, and we have a fair way to go before people start falling into generally accepted best practices. The Polymer (*https://www.polymer-project.org/*) group is leading the way, with Mozilla (*http://x-tags.org/*) having its own spin, and individuals in the community are adding in their own opinions as web components start being adopted in real-world applications.

In this environment, we felt that the greatest tool that we could put in the hands of developers interested in web components was an understanding of how to develop facets of the user interface (UI) in a reusable manner that can also translate directly to web components if (and when) you decide to use them.

In this book we'll be tackling the UI aspects for a common JavaScript widget, the dialog box. We'll go from basic creation to a vanilla web component, and then look at using Polymer to abstract it, build it, and deploy it as a reusable custom HTML element.

One of the biggest takeaways we want you to have after reading this book is that the introduction of web components, while it changes so much, doesn't remove the need to know and understand how to write modern JavaScript, and it doesn't invalidate the plethora of libraries and practices we've come to rely on and appreciate as part of frontend web development. With that said, web components certainly are a fresh and exciting way of tackling encapsulated logic and user interfaces and the landscape is full of innovation and opportunity.

Choose Your Own Adventure

This book is broken into four parts, allowing you to begin reading about the particular subject that most interests you. Are you already familiar with the concepts in Part I, *UI Core Concepts*? Then skip ahead to Part II, *Building Our UI*. Not interested in learning UI component implementation details and how to construct a dialog component? Then dive right into Part III, *Building HTML5 Web Components*, and learn all about this new technology. Already know about web components and are itching to learn how to use them in production applications? Then Part IV, *Testing, Building, and Deploying Components with Polymer* is for you. Where you begin and end is entirely up to you, and we wish you success on your adventure!

What Are Web Components?

"Web components" aren't any one thing; this is the term used for a collection of technologies that enable developers to effectively describe the implementations of HTML elements that already exist.

What does that even mean?

Well, if given the task of implementing a `<p>` tag via some other combination of HTML, JavaScript, and CSS, how would you do it? You could reasonably assume that the `<p>` tag just describes a set of styles and then maybe write a `<div>` with some inline style, or maybe a p class that groups paragraph styles together.

Now how would you implement, say, a `<select>` tag and its constituent list of `<option>` tags? That starts to get more complicated. It's doable, sure, but it's going to start being a hairy mess of styles, JavaScript, and HTML. Then consider how fragile the implementation would be. The styles may collide with the using page, as may classes, IDs, global JavaScript, etc. Again, it's doable, and we have done it, but it's far from ideal.

Further down that same path, how would you implement the `<video>` tag? This starts getting dicier and dicier, and these are the types of problems that web components technologies seek to solve. They don't go all the way, but they give developers a standard way to encapsulate, protect, and package these concepts.

Even if you don't think web components are the bee's knees (which they are, to the extent to which a bee's knees could possibly make web development a lot more satisfying and exciting), the constituent technologies are all independently useful and will undoubtedly find their way into frameworks like Angular and Ember, so they are worth being aware of and understanding.

What's intriguing about web components is that the bulk of it is maddeningly obvious. Two years after you buy into web components whole hog, you will look back at the twenty-aughts as this primitive time filled with Neanderlithic frameworks and "best practices" that involved putting whole string templates in <script> tags. When recalling this era of development to your grandchildren, they will look at you with skepticism and ask disbelievingly, "Gramps, did you *really* not have native templates in your DOM or are you just yanking our chains?"

And you'll say: "It's true, sweet Becca and little Johnny—now go play with your robots and don't touch my space bike."

Following is a rundown of some of the key areas we'll be exploring in this book.

HTML Templates

HTML templates are the simple embodiment of a templatized, inert Document Object Model (DOM) that can be stamped out and reused over and over again. Before the <template> tag, there existed any number of ways that you could reuse HTML. You could write your own functions that created and populated DOM nodes directly via DOM methods, you could retrieve text stored in the DOM via innerHTML and run that through a template engine, you could "precompile" templates in the build phase and send template functions, or you could choose some other equally uncomfortable method.

Now it's all over. There is one way to write reusable HTML. Its usage can certainly differ, but one thing's for sure: you're going to be writing your templates and partials in <template> tags from now on.

HTML Imports

The HTML import is another foolishly simple concept that accommodates a single interaction point for independent bundles to be loaded by. What has already been done for <script> and <style> tags has now been done for HTML itself. The bonus, on top of what was done for scripts and styles, is that the imported HTML can then infinitely link to all its own dependencies in the same formats that already exist. This will allow a developer to include miniature applications and all their dependencies with a single @include, instead of tracking everything down and including all the sources or links directly.

Custom Elements

Finally! There now exists a standard way of generating custom elements across framework, platform, and all other boundaries. The core of HTML, the single element, is now open to everyone. The custom element API is incredibly trivial, and it's meant to be. This is the first step to building HTML into what our apps have always wanted to be. This is about far more than simply creating new textual tags; it's opening up a strict API touchpoint that everyone is inherently familiar with. It's a contract that is already agreed upon, tolerated, and enjoyed by every web developer that exists.

The Shadow DOM

The shadow DOM is the secret sauce to web components. Each other technology on its own provides value that is obvious and appreciated, but the shadow DOM is the icing on the web component waffle. It finally provides a way for us to isolate portions of the DOM for true protection from styling, access, and modification via common means. For anyone who has ever tried to build reusable UIs, this is a welcome change that could nearly bring a tear to the eye of the most jaded developer.

Combining each of these things, we have the ability to generate custom elements, generating their own subtrees that are isolated from the parent DOM, all importable via a single tag!

If we sound excited, it's because development with web components is like breathing fresh air after being in a coal mine for two decades. Like standing up after 50 pounds of weight have been removed from your back. It's a freedom that is welcome and genuinely exciting.

Why Web Components?

The Web is in a transitional state, and has been for quite some time. It was originally designed to view documents—that's why the applications we use to sift through its contents are called browsers! Since its inception, though, the Web has been slowly morphing into an application platform, radically transforming the software development landscape. It has never been easier to release a new version of an application: a developer pushes code changes or new assets to a server, and the end user refreshes the page (as someone once said, a page refresh is the "compile" of web development). Unfortunately, the browser has not kept pace with this revolution, forcing developers to come up with clever solutions to make the Web more of an application platform.

The past few years have seen the emergence of JavaScript Model-View-Controller (MVC) libraries and frameworks designed to help give web applications structure.

The JavaScript MVC libraries that have been released over the past few years have not all been strictly MVC. The acronym MV* was created to encompass other patterns, such as MVVM (*http://bit.ly/dwc-mvvm*) and MVP (*http://bit.ly/dwc-mvp*).

Module loaders such as Require.JS (*http://requirejs.org/*) have also helped greatly, providing more structure by supplying the equivalent (and more) of the missing import that is standard in other platforms. This has allowed frontend engineers to think more modularly. Before the rise of MVC, we saw the rise of jQuery and UI widget libraries. These libraries were developed to help normalize web development as much as possible and to fill in the gaps in the limited set of UI components available on the Web. Before these libraries, writing JavaScript that interacted with the DOM across browsers was a nightmare and simple forms were the only UI natively supported by the browsers.

If you step back and look objectively at the current state of web development, it is really a giant hack—but that has been changing in recent years.

The fact that it is a hack, in a sense, is not altogether bad. It has provided a sense of freedom that other platforms and languages lack. Irritating as it can be at times, it's hard to imagine developing in a more restrictive environment.

The emergence of HTML5 and newer APIs is evidence of a great attempt at turning the Web into a real application platform. However, it is still missing some important features that are in most other application platforms.

For instance, the Web is not extensible. You cannot create new types of elements or extend existing ones, and there are no imports or methods for encapsulating components. Enter web components.

The term "web components" is currently being thrown around in the same way as "HTML5." Both terms have different meanings for different people. Taken literally, HTML5 is simply a new document type with more elements. However, when people talk about HTML5 they are typically including the new elements, CSS3, and the new JavaScript APIs, which together redefine web development. The same is true of web components—the term is used to reference a new collection of features that, when utilized together, allow developers to create reusable components in a standard fashion.

Imagine a world in which the web platform is natively extensible. Any element can be extended, and new elements can be defined to easily create rich user interfaces. Also, imagine a world in which these extensions can be imported in a uniform fashion, including all assets such as JavaScript, CSS, and images. Imagine that this system has been optimized to deduplicate requests for the same import and that blocks of markup can be loaded and marked as inert so as not to impact performance. Imagine a real application platform, if you will. This is the promise of web components.

What if you could create a dialog component simply by importing the resource and declaring meaningful markup?

```html
<head>
    <link rel="import" href="/imports/dialog/index.html">
</head>
<body>
    <dialog-component title="After Ford">
        Ending is better than mending. <br />
        The more stitches, the less riches.
    </dialog-component>
</body>
```

That would be a huge improvement in terms of readability over the current standard:

```html
<!-- based on http://jqueryui.com/dialog/ -->
<head>
    <link
     rel="stylesheet"
     href="//code.jquery.com/ui/1.11.0/themes/smoothness/jquery-ui.css">
    <script src="//code.jquery.com/jquery-1.10.2.js"></script>
    <script src="//code.jquery.com/ui/1.11.0/jquery-ui.js"></script>
    <script>
        $(function () {
            $( "#dialog" ).dialog();
        });
    </script>
</head>
<body>
    <div id="dialog" title="After Ford">
        Ending is better than mending. <br />
        The more stitches, the less riches.
    </div>
</body>
```

This is not to say that current widget libraries do not have anything to offer or that their patterns are flawed. In fact, they are still quite relevant given the current browser support for web components. Additionally, the web components specification alone is not a panacea for creating rich user interfaces. A dialog component would still be driven by the same code as a dialog widget. However, the dialog component would wrap the widget code in a simplified, standardized, native interface with a convenient method for including its dependencies.

While this might not sound like a vast improvement, the ability to extend, abstract, import, and encapsulate natively will make the development of web applications much easier. It will allow developers to create reusable elements with standard life cycles that can be imported by any application. This standardization will form an implicit contract between the elements and the application, making the creation and management of interfaces a much smoother process.

PART I

UI Core Concepts

A solid foundation is the key to constructing a building that will withstand the abuses of nature over the course of time. The same is true for software, but the foundation is knowledge—a firm understanding of design concepts and implementation patterns—not concrete. Without this foundation, an engineer will inevitably create unstable software that eventually crumbles. The downfall may be code smell due to a misunderstanding of a core concept, a poor API resulting from an insufficient design period, poor implementation due to not knowing a standard pattern, etc. The intent of Part I is to help prevent this downfall.

These opening chapters are designed to help you create a better foundation by covering commonly misunderstood (or inadequately understood) concepts that are core to positioning, dragging, and resizing elements—core features required of most UI components. In addition to these concepts, basic design considerations are discussed to help ensure consistency across components and prevent common design mistakes.

If you already have this knowledge, then great—skip to Part II! If you want a refresher, then just skim Part I. If you want to understand the base component class that will be used throughout the book, then just read the last section of Chapter 2 ("Example Widget" on page 18). Remember, this is your adventure!

Throughout Parts I and II of this book, the term *widget* will be used when referring to different libraries and the dialog example. You might find yourself asking, "Why are we building a widget? I thought this was a web components book!" That's a valid question. The answer is that this book is more than just a rehashing of the Web Components specification. It is designed to provide a better understanding of the DOM by exploring the details underlying today's widget interfaces. Knowledge of these details is required to build moderately complex web components, and what better way to understand these details than through a concrete example?

CHAPTER 2

Creating a Solid Foundation

Jason Strimpel

Before learning about and developing web components, there are a few things that you should consider. Some of these considerations are not unique to web components, but rather are important aspects of software design and frontend engineering in general.

Voltron—The Component Base Class

In this chapter we will be constructing a base class widget, *Voltron*. This widget will be used to construct a dialog widget that will be iteratively built throughout this book as new concepts are introduced. The purpose of this base widget is to provide a standard that can be leveraged for the construction of a DOM library, irrespective of the interface—JavaScript widget, pure web component, Polymer, etc.

The Importance of a DOM Abstraction Layer

In theory, the DOM and its API provide a good interface for working with an HTML document. However, in practice it can be a very frustrating interface. This is especially true across browsers. In his book *Learning JavaScript Design Patterns* (*http://bit.ly/ZQNe8L*) (O'Reilly), Addy Osmani describes how jQuery abstracts away the details of element selection, specifically selecting elements by class name. It accomplishes this by providing a convenient facade, its query selector API. Selecting an element by class name can be done in one of three ways, and the method selected is dependent upon what the browser running jQuery supports. jQuery hides these details and automatically selects the most efficient method. In addition to abstracting away these types of details, a good DOM library provides convenient APIs for common traversal and manipulation use cases.

The examples in this book will utilize jQuery, since it is known and used by a larger audience than any other DOM facade library.

Suppose you wanted to find the closest ancestor element with a given tag name and set the text color for that node to red. Using native APIs this could be accomplished as follows:

```
function colorize(el, tagName) {
    // get el's parent el/node
    var parentEl = el.parentNode;
    // ensure tag name passed is uppercase
    tagName = tagName.toUpperCase();

    // loop through ancestors starting with
    // the el's parent until the node tag name
    // matches the tagName argument or 'HTML'
    while (parentEl.tagName !== 'HTML') {
        if (parentEl.tagName === tagName) {
            parentEl.style.color = '#ff0000';
            break;
        }
        parentEl = parentEl.parentNode;
    }
}

// get the element with an id of 'descendant' and set
// closest ancestor div's color to red
colorize(document.getElementById('descendant'), 'DIV');
```

Using jQuery this can be accomplished in a much more concise manner, and any valid query selectors can be used to match the elements, not just the tag name:

```
// get the element with an id of 'descendant' and set
// closest ancestor div's color to red
$('#descendant').closest('div').css({ 'color': '#ff0000' });
```

You do not want to have to continuously write these types of abstractions and unearth all the cross-browser oddities yourself, unless you intend to create the next jQuery!

API Design and Widget Life Cycle

Before writing a single line of code, you should have a rough idea of what your API will look like and a basic understanding of how your widget life cycle will flow. Without a consistent API and a common life cycle, others will not be able to easily utilize your widget library, and eventually you will find it difficult to work with your own library if you step away from the code for more than a day or two.

A widget life cycle consists of, but is not limited to, initialization, rendering, event bindings, and destruction. The jQuery UI and the widget factory (*https://jqueryui.com/widget/*) are excellent examples of well-defined life cycle management.

A good example of the need for API and life cycle consistency is how a widget cleans up after itself. Anyone who has worked with jQuery plugins written by different authors knows just how frustrating this can be. Some have a "destroy" method. Others have a "remove" method. Some do not even account for cleanup. None of them seem to follow a common pattern or have the same behavior. This makes cleaning up from a parent widget or object much more difficult, because there is no common API to fall back on. The following code block is an example stub for a life cycle that will be used for widgets in this book:

```
// utility function for enabling and disabling element
function disable ($el, disabled) {
    this.$el[disabled ? 'addClass' : 'removeClass']('disabled')
        .find('input, textarea, select, button')
        .prop('disabled', disabled);
}

// constructor function for creating an instance of a widget
function WidgetName (options) {
    this.options = $.extend({}, this.defaults, options);
    // initialize widget
    this.init();
    // return reference to instance
    return this;
}

// options defaults
WidgetName.prototype.defaults = {
    width: 200 // example option
};

// placeholder for widget initialization logic
WidgetName.prototype.init = function () {
    this.$el = $(options.$el);
    this.bind();
};

// placeholder for rendering logic
WidgetName.prototype.render = function () {
    // appropriate events could be triggered here and in other methods, e.g.
    this.$el.trigger('rendered', [this]);
    return this;
};

// bind events using delegation and namespace
```

```
WidgetName.prototype.bind = function () {
    this.$el.on('click.cmp-name', function (e) {});
    return this;
};

// unbind events
WidgetName.prototype.unbind = function () {
    this.$el.off('click.cmp-name');
    return this;
};

// placeholder disabling a widget
WidgetName.prototype.disable = function () {
    disable(this.$el, true);
    return this;
};

// placeholder enabling a widget
WidgetName.prototype.enable = function () {
    disable(this.$el, false);
    return this;
};

// custom cleanup logic can be added here
WidgetName.prototype.destroy = function () {
    this.unbind();
    this.$el.remove();
};
```

Whatever names you select for your API methods, and however you decide the life cycle should flow, just *be consistent*! Most developers would much rather work with an API that is slightly less descriptive, but consistent, than with a self-describing API that behaves erratically.

Additionally, a good API should provide sensible defaults and hook points with useful function arguments so that developers can easily override methods to meet their needs without affecting the life cycle.

Lastly, not everything is a jQuery plugin! Your API design should not start with `$.fn.*`. You should have a solid API design and adopt a sensible inheritance pattern. Then, if it makes sense, you can turn your widget into a jQuery plugin to make it easier for others to consume.

The Inheritance Pattern

JavaScript uses prototypal inheritance (*http://bit.ly/dwc-proto*). This often confuses engineers who are transitioning over from other languages because in prototypal inheritance objects inherit directly from other objects, as opposed to classical inheritance, where a new instance is created from a class that is essentially a blueprint for

---

creating an object. Initially, most view JavaScript as inferior to statically typed languages that use classical inheritance. I am not going debate the finer points, but in my opinion JavaScript is more flexible because it allows engineers to implement inheritance patterns of their choosing. Personally, I am a fan of Backbone's inheritance pattern (*http://bit.ly/dwc-backbone-ip*), which was inspired by `goog.inherits` from Google Closure (*http://bit.ly/dwc-closure*), because it abstracts away the mechanism of inheritance, allowing developers to focus on creating objects. Additionally, it implements constructs with which most developers are familiar: instance properties, static properties, and access to super properties.

The examples in this book will use a simple constructor pattern as to not detract from the main focus of the book, developing web components:

```
// base class constructor
function BaseWidget(options) {
    // see previous code example on life cycles
    // for an explaination of the line below
    this.options = augment(this.defaults, options);
}

// extend base class
SubClassWidget.prototype = new BaseWidget();
SubClassWidget.prototype.constructor = SubClassWidget;
function SubClassWidget(options) {
    BaseWidget.call(this, options);
}
```

Dependencies

When creating a web widget, you should always do your best to limit dependencies on other modules. I am not advocating against DRY or code reuse; I'm just saying that you should evaluate whether adding a library as a dependency is providing value that is worth its weight in terms of file size and maintenance, and the dependency burden it will place on consumers of your widget. The examples in this book will rely on jQuery only. Each example will pass dependencies into a closure. For instance:

```
(function (root, $) {
    // widget awesomeness goes here
})(window, jQuery);
```

When creating any JavaScript module that will be used by a large audience, it is best to offer alternate formats for including your module. For instance, I always create an AMD version. If the code runs on both the client and the server, then I ensure it is possible to easily include the code via CommonJS, so it can be run in Node.js.

The Asynchronous Module Definition (AMD) (*http://bit.ly/dwc-amd*) API specifies a mechanism for defining modules such that the module and its dependencies can be loaded asynchronously. This is particularly well suited for the browser environment, where synchronous loading of modules incurs performance, usability, debugging, and cross-domain access problems.

The following examples use Grunt (*http://gruntjs.com*) to build the files via Jarrod Overson's `grunt-preprocess` plugin (*http://bit.ly/dwc-grunt-preprocess*):

```
// https://github.com/jstrimpel/hermes/blob/master/src/hermes.amd.js
define(function () {

    'use strict';

    // @include hermes.js

    return hermes;

});
```

```
// https://github.com/jstrimpel/hermes/blob/master/src/hermes.window.js
(function (window) {

    'use strict';

    // @include hermes.js

    window.hermes = window.hermes || hermes;

})(window);
```

Optimization

Donald Knuth once said, "Premature optimization is the root of all evil." I have never known a statement to ring truer and as frequently in software engineering. I cannot count how many times I have seen prematurely optimizing code introduce bugs.

People frequently advocate caching jQuery objects, which is a practice I am not against in principle. But imagine you have a node that is destroyed because a widget component has completely replaced its inner HTML by redrawing itself via a template. You now have a reference to an orphaned node. This orphaned node cannot be garbage collected, and your application has a memory leak. It is a small leak, but if you are applying the same pattern across all widgets, then it can become a much larger problem rather quickly. This is especially true if your application goes for an extended period of time without doing a hard refresh.

Aside from the leak, any code that was utilizing this reference to perform DOM manipulations is now broken. The obvious solution is to understand the entire life cycle of your application, but this becomes impossible once an application reaches a certain size. Even if you could keep track of the entire application, you are likely using third-party libraries. While these libraries provide great benefits by encapsulating solutions to common problems, they hide the implementation details of how they are manipulating the DOM.

Your design, life cycles, and API should be your first considerations. In the case of Voltron, our UI base widget, the specific primary considerations were rendering, UI (un)binding, and disabling, so we created a generic interface that could be extended to support these concepts. Additional concerns, common to most software components, were construction, inheritance, and initialization, so we used a well-known inheritance pattern and provided an extendable hook point for initialization. This allows us to periodically run performance tests as we are implementing the details the underlie the API.

> If you have a well-designed API, then you should be able to make optimizations on a case-by-case basis at a later date if significant performance bottlenecks are found.

The bottom line is to code sensibly by adhering to some best practices (like performing batch updates on the DOM), performance test as you implement your API, and then wait until a performance issue arises before further optimizing.

A Web Component Is Not JavaScript Alone

The first section of this book covers the JavaScript details of developing a web component, but web components are not solely comprised of JavaScript. If they were, then adopting a module format such as AMD or CommonJS, or simply using `<script>` tags, would make web components unnecessary. Web components attempt to solve a much larger problem, which is how to encapsulate HTML, CSS, and Java-Script, and make this encapsulation extensible without any impact on surrounding nodes in the DOM. For example, if a developer wants to create an image slider (*http://bit.ly/dwc-css-tricks*), it should be possible to do this in a declarative manner via a custom element in the document:

```
<!-- http://css-tricks.com/modular-future-web-components/ -->
<div class="img-slider">
  <img src="./rock.jpg" alt="an interesting rock">
  <img src="./grooves.jpg" alt="some neat grooves">
  <img src="./arch.jpg" alt="a rock arch">
```

```
    <img src="./sunset.jpg" alt="a dramatic sunset">
  </div>
```

The resources that support this custom element should be easily included in an import and the implementation details should not be a concern for the author of the document.

The realization of this encapsulated, declarative approach will transform the Web from a quasi development platform to a bona fide development platform.

Example Widget

A dialog widget will be constructed throughout the course of the book as new concepts are introduced in each chapter. The end result will be a fully functioning modal dialog that can be instantiated, initialized with data, moved, resized, and shown/hidden on demand. This example will include all the necessary CSS, HTML, and JavaScript.

The Voltron Widget Base Class

Typically, I create a base class for any object that creates instances of itself. The base class contains common methods that can be easily overridden by the classes that extend it. It also allows for easily calling the base class's `prototype` method.

We use classic object-oriented programming (OOP) terms such as "base" and "super" throughout the book. This is not because classic OOP in better than prototypal inheritance; it is because these terms provide a frame of reference for explaining concepts.

The base class for the Voltron widget looks like this:

```
// calling a base class method
Super.prototype.doSomething = function () {
    Base.prototype.doSomething.call(this);
    // now do some other stuff that is unique to the Super class
};

(function (root, $) {

    // https://github.com/jashkenas/backbone/blob/master/backbone.js#L1027
    // cached regex to split keys for `delegate`
    var delegateEventSplitter = /^(\S+)\s*(.*)$/;

    // constructor; creates instance
    function Voltron(options) {
        this.init(options);
        return this;
    }
```

```
// default options
Voltron.prototype.defaults = {};

// events hash
Voltron.prototype.events = {};

// initialization code
Voltron.prototype.init = function (options) {
    this.options = $.extend({}, this.defaults, options);
    this.$el = $(options.$el);
    this.bind();
    return this;
};

// heavily based on Backbone.View.delegateEvents
// https://github.com/jashkenas/backbone/blob/master/backbone.js#L1088
// bind using event delegation
Voltron.prototype.bind = function () {
    var events = this.options.events ? Voltron.result(this.options.events) :
        null;

    if (!events) {
        return this;
    }

    // prevent double binding of events
    this.unbind();

    // iterate over events hash
    for (var key in events) {
        var method = events[key];
        // if value is not a function then
        // find corresponding instance method
        if (!$.isFunction(method)) {
            method = this[events[key]];
        }
        // if a method does not exist move
        // to next item in the events hash
        if (!method) {
            continue;
        }

        // extract event name and selector from
        // property
        var match = key.match(delegateEventSplitter);
        var eventName = match[1];
        var selector = match[2];

        // bind event callback to widget instance
        method = $.proxy(method, this);
```

```
                if (selector.length) {
                    this.$el.on(eventName, selector, method);
                } else {
                    this.$el.on(eventName, method);
                }
            }
        };

        // used to unbind event handlers
        Voltron.prototype.unbind = function () {
            this.$el.off();
            return this;
        };

        // destroy instance
        Voltron.prototype.destroy = function () {
            this.unbind();
            this.$el.remove();
        };

        // static util method for returning a value
        // of an unknown type - if value is a function then execute
        // and return value of function
        Voltron.result = function (val) {
            return $.isFunction(val) ? val() : val;
        };

        window.Voltron = window.Voltron || Voltron;

    })(window, jQuery);
```

Dialog Class

The dialog widget will extend the Voltron base class example from the previous section. The source code that follows is the stub for the dialog widget, which will be filled in progressively over the next two chapters:

```
(function () {

    'use strict';

    // set prototype to base widget and assign
    // Dialog constructor to the constructor prototype
    Dialog.prototype = new Voltron({});
    Dialog.prototype.constructor = Dialog;

    // constructor
    function Dialog (options) {
        Voltron.call(this, options);
        return this;
```

```
    }

    // defaults, e.g., width and height
    Dialog.prototype.defaults = {};

    // event listeners; this is processed by Voltron.prototype.bind
    Dialog.prototype.events = {};

    // process template for injection into DOM
    Dialog.prototype.render = function () {};

    // makes dialog visible in the UI
    Dialog.prototype.show = function () {};

    // makes dialog invisible in the UI
    Dialog.prototype.hide = function () {};

    window.Dialog = window.Dialog || Dialog;

})(window, jQuery, Voltron);
```

Dialog CSS and HTML

The HTML and CSS that follows is intended to provide the basic structure for rendering the dialog widget:

```
<div role="dialog" aria-labelledby="title" aria-describedby="content">
    <h2 id="title">Dialog Title</h2>
    <p id="content">I am the dialog content.</p>
</div>
[role="dialog"] {
    width: 400px;
    height: 200px;
    position: absolute;
}

[role="dialog"] h2 {
    background: #ccc;
    font-size: 16px;
    font-weight: normal;
    padding: 10px;
    margin: 0;
}

[role="dialog"] p {
    margin: 0;
    padding: 10px;
    font-size: 12px;
}
```

Summary

In this chapter we covered the productivity and normalization benefits of a DOM abstraction library and selected a well-known library, jQuery, as the library to be used throughout the course of the book. We then discussed how defining a common life cycle and base class can help make applications easier to develop, maintain, and debug because it helps define expected outcomes and behaviors. Next we explored how to include library dependencies and described a common inheritance pattern that will be used throughout the book. Finally, we created Voltron, the base class widget, and extended it to create the dialog widget, which will be iteratively built in the following chapters to turn concepts into a working component. You now have the necessary knowledge to begin your web components journey!

CHAPTER 3

Normal Flow and Positioning

Jason Strimpel

Every web component will be appended to the DOM and ultimately rendered to the screen for users to interact with. Understanding where and how an element, the building block of a web component, is positioned is key to developing web components.

Not understanding fundamental layout concepts can have a great impact on your web component's design and implementation. For instance, depending on the requirements, a modal dialog can be rendered by calculating its size relative to the viewport and positioning it absolutely, or a simpler technique using fixed positioning and margins can be utilized. The latter technique uses pure CSS to do the positioning, so it performs much better, and the likelihood of bugs is decreased because you are doing significantly less DOM manipulation via JavaScript.

The two key concepts for understanding how the browser lays out a page are normal flow and positioning.

Normal Flow

The browser renders elements by placing them on a page according to what is known as *normal flow*.

Per the W3C CSS 2.1 specification (*http://bit.ly/dwc-normal-flow*):

> Boxes in the normal flow belong to a formatting context, which may be block or inline, but not both simultaneously. Block-level boxes participate in a block formatting context. Inline-level boxes participate in an inline formatting context.

Let's translate this W3C-speak into something someone other than a browser developer can understand.

"Boxes" refers to the box model (*http://bit.ly/dwc-box*), which describes how boxes represent elements. Every element on the page is a box composed of pixels. Boxes have properties such as padding, margins, and borders that, combined with the box content, determine how much space an element will occupy on a page. There are other properties, like box-sizing (*http://bit.ly/dwc-box-sz*) and the document type (in older versions of Internet Explorer), that can impact how these rules are interpreted and the resulting space occupied, but for the most part it a very simple model.

Block (*http://bit.ly/dwc-block*) elements flow vertically (stacked one on top of the other) and fill their parent container if a width is not set. Inline (*http://bit.ly/dwc-inline*) elements flow horizontally (side by side) and occupy only as much width as the box context, left and right margins, and padding require. Figure 3-1 illustrates the difference. Setting the width and height on an inline element does not have any effect on the space it occupies.

Figure 3-1. An inline element occupies only as much width as its content requires, while a block element occupies the full width of its containing element unless a specific width value is set

This is how elements normally flow within a document, if specific position values are not applied.

Positioning Elements

In the normal flow, an element's default position value is static. A static element is technically not positioned. A positioned element is said to have a position value of relative, absolute, or fixed, and it is removed from the normal flow:

```
<!-- not positioned -->
<div>Some amazing text</div>

<!-- positioned -->
<div style="position: relative">Some amazing text</div>
```

 Positioning does not cascade (i.e., it is not inherited by child elements), so you have to specifically set it on an element. Otherwise, the default value of static will be applied.

offsetParent

When an element is positioned, it is considered to be a *containing element*. A containing element is a reference point for positioning child elements using the top, right, bottom, and/or left properties. This containing element then becomes the offsetParent (*http://bit.ly/dwc-offsetparent*) for its child elements and any ancestors of the children that are not descendants of closer-positioned ancestors. Figure 3-2 illustrates the effects of different position values.

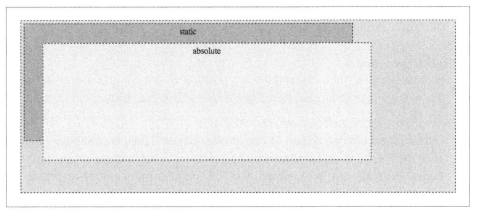

Figure 3-2. A relative-positioned containing element with a static element and an absolute-positioned element that has top and left values of 40px

How the browser determines an element's offsetParent

An element's offsetParent property can be either null, the <body>, or an ancestor element other than the <body>. The browser uses the W3C specification (*http://bit.ly/dwc-w3c-op*) to determine an element's offsetParent value, as follows:

offsetParent *is* null

> Occasionally, an element's offsetParent value will be null. This occurs when the element is the <body>, when the element does not have a layout box (i.e., its display is none) and when the element has not been appended to the DOM. The offsetParent will also be null if the element's position is fixed because it is positioned relative to the viewport, not another element. The following example illustrates these cases:

```
<div id="div1" style="display: none"></div>
<div id="div2" style="position: fixed"></div>

var $body = $('body');
console.log($body.offsetParent()[0]); // logs <html>
console.log($body[0].offsetParent); // logs null

var $div1 = $('#div1');
```

```
console.log($div1.offsetParent()[0]); // logs <html>
console.log($div1[0].offsetParent); // logs null

var $div2 = $('#div2');
console.log($div2.offsetParent()[0]); // logs <html>
console.log($div2[0].offsetParent); // logs null
```

 While the value of offsetParent can be null, the return value from jQuery's offsetParent method is never null. jQuery returns <html> as the offsetParent, ensuring that there is always an element against which to operate.

offsetParent *is* <body>

If the element is not a descendant of a positioned element and it does not meet any of the null criteria, then its offsetParent will be the <body>.

offsetParent *is an ancestor element other than* <body>

If the element is a descendant of a positioned element, then the closest positioned ancestor will be its offsetParent. If an element is not a descendant of a positioned element but is a descendant of <td>, <th>, or <table>, then its offsetParent will be the closest of the aforementioned tags.

Positioning

Positioning is frequently misunderstood. Often developers will set a different posi tion value on an element in an attempt to fix a layout when things are not looking quite right. While this approach can "fix" a layout, it does not promote an understanding of how positioning actually works. Having a firm grasp of positioning can save you a great deal of time in the long run, because once you understand how it works you will begin to construct pages in a much more efficient manner.

Relative positioning

When an element is positioned relatively, the space it would have occupied in the normal flow is reserved. All other elements in the normal flow render around the space as if the element were in the normal flow. Visually, it is placed as if its position value were static. However, as Figure 3-3 illustrates, unlike with a static element, setting the top, right, bottom, or left values will shift the element accordingly. Positioning an element relatively is typically done to create a containing element for positioning child elements, or to apply a z-index (z-index is not applicable to statically positioned elements). Relative positioning is assigned as follows:

```
.some-class-selector {
    position: relative;
}
```

Think of *relative* as being relative to the element and the space it occupies in the normal flow.

Figure 3-3. A relatively positioned element with top and left values of 10px—note that the space it would have occupied in the normal flow remains intact

Absolute positioning

When an element is positioned absolutely, it is taken out of the normal flow of the document and the space the element would have occupied collapses (see Figure 3-4). The element can then be positioned by setting the `top`, `right`, `bottom`, and `left` values. Absolute positioning is useful for creating components such as tooltips, overlays, or anything that should be positioned at a precise location outside of the normal flow.

Figure 3-4. An absolutely positioned element with an opacity of 0.75 and top and left values of 75px—note that the space it would have occupied in the normal flow collapses

Fixed positioning

An element is also taken out of the normal flow of the document when its position is fixed. It is positioned relative to the viewport, not the document, so when the page is scrolled the element remains fixed in place as if it were part of the viewport itself. This is useful for creating sticky headers and footers, and modal overlays. Here's an example:

```
/*
Covers the viewport when applied to an
element that is a child of the <body>.
It stretches the element across the <body> by
fixing its position and setting all the position
properties to 0. This makes it impossible to
interact with any elements that are in lower rendering
layers.
*/
.modal-overlay {
    position: fixed;
    top: 0;
    left: 0;
    right: 0;
    bottom: 0;
    background: #000;
    opacity: .5;
}

/*
Centers an element in the viewport by setting the top and left
properties to 50%. It then accounts for the height and width of the element
by taking half the height and width, and sets the top and left properties
respectively by negating these values.
*/
.modal-content {
    position: fixed;
```

```
        top:50%;
        left:50%;
        margin-top: -100px;
        margin-left: -200px;
        width: 400px;
        height: 200px;
        background: #fff;
        padding: 10px;
        overflow: auto;
    }

    <div class="modal-overlay"></div>
    <div class="modal-content">I am the modal content. Fear me.</div>
```

Calculating an Element's Position

In addition to understanding positioning, it is important to know how to get an element's position relative to the viewport and the document. This is useful for positioning elements relative to each other when creating components such as tooltips, dialogs, sliders, etc.

Relative to the Viewport

Getting an element's position relative to the viewport alone is typically not that useful. Most of the time you want the element's position relative to the document, so you can absolutely position another element next to it.

However, the method used to retrieve the position relative to the viewport, `ele ment.getBoundingClientRect` (*http://bit.ly/dwc-gbcr*), returns the top, right, bottom, and left values, which allows you to easily calculate an element's width and height. This information, in conjunction with an element's position relative to the document, is useful when creating components that need to align with another element or be constrained by another element's size, such as drop-downs or tooltips.

Alternatively, you could just use `$.outerWidth` (*http://bit.ly/dwc-outerw*) and `$.outer Height` (*http://bit.ly/dwc-outerh*) to obtain an element's dimensions, but `element.getBoundingClientRect` is significantly faster (*http://bit.ly/dwc-vs*). Also, `element.getBoundingClientRect` can be used with a couple of other properties to quickly look up an element's position relative to the document:

```
    <body>
    ...
        <form>
        ...
            <input name="fname" />
        ...
        </form>
    ...
    </body>
```

```
var $input = $('[name="fname"]');
var rect = $input[0].getBoundingClientRect();
```

Relative to the Document

Getting an element's position relative to the document is useful for absolutely positioning an element so that it remains positioned as the page scrolls, and for positioning elements relative to each other within the document. It is a fairly straightforward process. You traverse the DOM, finding each offsetParent, and get its offsetLeft and offsetTop. These values are the offset from the next offsetParent, so you have to sum the values until you reach the <body>:

```
function getElOffsets(el) {
    var offsets = {
        left: el.offsetLeft || 0,
        top: el.offsetTop || 0
    };

    // loop through ancestors while ancestor is an offsetParent
    while (el = el.offsetParent) {
        // sum the offset values
        offsets.left += el.offsetLeft || 0;
        offsets.top += el.offsetTop || 0;
    }

    return offsets;
}
```

A quick Internet search for "JavaScript get element position relative to the body" will result in numerous examples that are roughly the same as the one outlined here. However, there is a much better way of doing this in conjunction with element.get BoundingClientRect, courtesy of jQuery:

```
// https://github.com/jquery/jquery/blob/master/src/offset.js#L105
// box is the el.getBoundingClientRect()
// win is the window object
// docElem is <html> (see
// https://developer.mozilla.org/en-US/docs/Web/API/document.documentElement)
//
// calculating left and top return values
// 1. get the distance of top or bottom from the viewport
// 2. get the distance between the viewport top or left from the top of the page
//    & add it to the value from distance of top or bottom from the viewport
// 3. subtract any top or left offsets of <html>, e.g., margins
offset: function( options ) {
...
    return {
                top: box.top + win.pageYOffset - docElem.clientTop,
                left: box.left + win.pageXOffset - docElem.clientLeft
            };
}
```

I recommend just using `$.offset` (*http://api.jquery.com/offset/*) as it performs consistently across browsers, and jQuery has been well tested and vetted by a very large user community. `$.offset` is an excellent example of the benefits of using a DOM manipulation library: you get the collective intelligence of a community wrapped up in a nice API.

Positioning the Dialog Widget

The dialog widget will need to be absolutely positioned, so that it can be removed from the normal flow and not impact the page's layout. Ignoring all other factors, such as the dialog element's location in the DOM tree, this is very easy to accomplish:

```
function Dialog (options) {
    // call superclass constructor
    Voltron.call(this, options);
    return this;
}

Dialog.prototype.init = function (options) {
    // call super method
    Voltron.prototype.init.call(this, options);
    // position the dialog's root element absolutely
    this.$el.css({ position: 'absolute' });
};
```

Summary

In this chapter we examined the importance of understanding normal flow and positioning, and specifically how having a firm understanding of these concepts can significantly improve the design and performance of a component (e.g., using JavaScript versus pure CSS to position a dialog). As part of this examination we reviewed the box model and the two main types of boxes, block and inline. Next we covered the different types of positioning: relative, absolute, and fixed. After that we discussed how the browser positions an element and how to determine a positioned element's `offsetParent`. Finally, we applied this knowledge to the dialog widget.

Understanding and Managing z-index

Jason Strimpel

How many times have you seen CSS similar to the following?

```
.some-selector {
    position: relative;
    z-index: 3870814; /* do NOT change!!! */
}
```

It is probably safe to assume that the element in question is not competing with 3,800,000+ elements to be the top element on the page. If so, the developer has an amazing mental map of a massive page that would likely crash any browser!

Typically when you encounter CSS and comments like these it is because there was confusion not about the z-index property and value itself, but rather about the other factors that contribute to the stacking order of an element on a page—stacking contexts, positioning, opacity, etc.

Certain steps can be taken to prevent CSS and comments like those in the previous example, but first one must have a solid understanding of the z-index property and all the contributing factors that ultimately determine how elements are layered.

What Exactly Is the z-index Property?

Per the W3C, the z-index (*http://bit.ly/dwc-zindex*) property is used to specify:

1. The stack level of the box in the current stacking context
2. Whether the box establishes a stacking context

The W3C definition is concise and accurate. However, the definition assumes knowledge of stacking contexts, which is not an introductory z-index topic. The W3C also provides an elaborate explanation (*http://bit.ly/dwc-stacking*) of stacking contexts. This information, while accurate, does not make a good basis for fully understanding the z-index property unless you already have intimate knowledge of other specifications that describe how a browser renders a page. A better place to begin understanding z-index is to first understand rendering layers and stacking order.

Rendering Layers, Stacking Order, and z-index

The previous chapter introduced normal flow and described how elements are rendered in the normal flow. It also described how positioned elements are taken out of the normal flow. The removal of positioned elements from the normal flow is an excellent starting point for understanding z-index because it is related to the concept of rendering layers.

A web page is often thought of in terms of two dimensions: the horizontal axis, x, and the vertical axis, y. However, there is a third dimension, which is the z-axis. The z-index value of an element represents the layer in which the element is rendered on the z-axis.

The default rendering layer (z-axis) is 0. Setting a negative z-index value places the rendering layer behind the default rendering layer, making it "invisible." This technique is often used for performing calculations on an element that the developer does not want the user to see, but that require an element to have dimensions.

When an element is positioned, it is removed from the normal flow but remains in the same rendering layer. The positioning impacts the element's placement in the stacking order.

Default Stacking Orders

Elements without a z-index are positioned in order from bottom to top within a stacking context as follows:

1. Background and borders of the root element

2. Descendant blocks in the normal flow, in order of appearance (in HTML)

3. Descendant positioned elements, in order of appearance (in HTML)

Figure 4-1 illustrates the default stacking order for various positioned and nonpositioned elements.

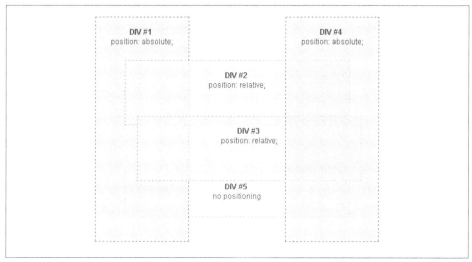

Figure 4-1. Default stacking order for positioned and nonpositioned elements (source: http://bit.ly/dwc-stacking-z)

The default stacking order must also take *floated elements* into account. Floated elements are stacked between non-positioned (static) elements, and positioned elements. Figure 4-2 shows how they fit into the default stacking order.

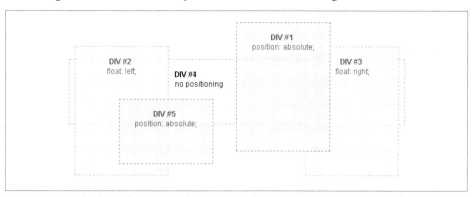

Figure 4-2. Default stacking order for positioned, nonpositioned, and floated elements (source: http://bit.ly/dwc-stackfloat-z)

Overriding the Default Stacking Order

z-index is used to specify a stacking order other than the default. To move an element closer to the top of the stack (i.e., visually closer to the user), a positive integer value is assigned to the z-index property of the element. If no other values in the same stacking context have a z-index property, then a value of 1 will move an element to the top. If other elements have z-index values assigned to them, then a value higher than the highest z-index value in the same stacking context will place the element at the top of the stack. A negative value will position an element below the default rendering layer.

Elements with the same z-index follow the default stacking rules.

Seems pretty simple, right? If you read the last paragraph carefully, though, you will notice that there was always a qualifying condition to the effect of the z-index value: the elements must be within the same stacking context.

z-index only has an effect on positioned elements.

Stacking Contexts

The default stacking order and the effects of z-index values apply only to child elements of the element that creates a stacking context. Figure 4-3 shows an example of a stacking context with nested elements. Note how <div> 1 overlays <div> 4, even though it has a lower z-index value.

How Is a Stacking Context Created?

The default stacking context is the root element, <html>. A stacking context is created when an element is positioned and assigned a z-index value other than auto, or when an element has an opacity value less than 1. In WebKit and Chrome 22+ an element with a fixed position always creates a stacking context, even when the z-index value is auto. In addition to these properties and values, newer CSS properties and values, such as transform with a value other than none, also create stacking contexts.

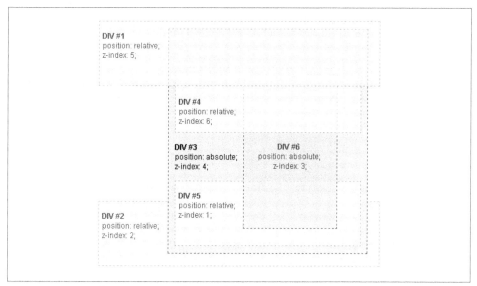

Figure 4-3. A stacking context with nested elements (source: http://bit.ly/dwc-stacking-context)

It is helpful to think of stacking contexts as establishing a new page in the sense that they have a self-contained normal flow and rendering layers.

Increasing Complexity

The significance of stacking contexts is that they create an independent set of rendering layers that are not impacted by the default stacking orders and z-index values of elements that reside outside them. In a simple web page stacking contexts usually are not a concern because there is often only one stacking context: the root element, <html>. However, as an interface becomes more sophisticated—e.g., as richer UI controls (dialogs, sliders, tooltips, etc.) are added—the likelihood of multiple stacking contexts existing increases. As more stacking contexts are introduced, the complexity of z-index management increases.

Managing z-indexes

A common approach to minimizing the z-index complexities that arise in dynamic web applications is to assign ranges to different types of controls. For example, if you look at some web advertising specifications, they provide ranges for different layers to help ensure that the layer in question is placed on top. The Interactive Advertising

Bureau (IAB) `z-index` guidelines (*http://bit.ly/dwc-guidelines*) are reproduced in Table 4-1, to give you an idea of what these guidelines may look like.

Table 4-1. IAB Display Advertising z-index Guidelines

Z-Index Range	Content Type	Details
< 0	Background Elements	
0 - 4,999	Main Content, Standard Ads	Standard ad tags in place with regular content. Includes OBA Self Regulation Message (CLEAR Ad Notice)
5,000 - 1,999,999	Expanding Advertising	The entire expandable ad unit should be set within this range
2,000,000 - 2,999,999	Floating Advertising	Over The Page ads (OTP's)
3,000,000 - 3,999,999	Pop-up Elements	Chat windows, message notifications
4,000,000 - 4,999,999	Non-anchored Floating Elements	Survey recruitment panels
5,000,000 - 5,999,999	Expanding Site Navigation Elements	Drop down navigation, site warnings, etc. Only the expanding portion of navigation elements should be included on this level.
6,000,000+	Full-page Overlays	Full-window Over-the-Page (OTP) ads and Between-the-Page ads IF they cover page content

This approach works well in less dynamic environments, such as ecommerce sites, but it falls short in web applications where the DOM and `z-index` values are constantly being modified by application-layer JavaScript and third-party plugins. A more reliable approach is to take your knowledge of `z-indexes` and manage them programmatically within your components and application code, in addition to assigning ranges to larger, static containers such as `<header>`, `<footer>`, `<aside>`, and `<article>` elements, or other logical groupings that makes sense within the context of your application.

z-index Manager

This section will cover the creation of a `z-index` manager. The manager will have the ability to send an element to the front or the back of a stacking context, get an element's stacking context, and determine if an element creates a stacking context.

API stub

The first step I always take when creating a new component is stubbing out an API. I then use this as a guide for implementing the functionality. Here, we'll create a z-index manager called Jenga:

```
// from this point forward all code examples will assume this closure
// and that jenga will be a property on the global window object
//
// AMD and jQuery versions are available at https://github.com/jstrimpel/jenga
var jenga = (function (global) {

    'use strict';

    return {

        isStackingCtx: function (el) {},

        getStackingCtx: function (el) {},

        bringToFront: function (el, createStackingCtx, root) {},

        sendToBack: function (el, createStackingCtx, root) {}
    };

})(this);
```

Utilities

Before stacking contexts can be determined and z-indexes managed, functions for identifying properties that create stacking contexts need to be written. This is done for reusage and to make the code that relies on these functions easier to read.

The rules for determining stacking contexts vary across browsers and browser versions. Accounting for these variations using feature detection (*http://bit.ly/dwc-feature-detection*) would be next to impossible to maintain, because the implementation across browsers is constantly in flux. For this reason, the z-index manager utilizes browser detection:

```
// this will be used for addressing all the browser- & version-specific
// items that impact stacking contexts
// fixed - the version where position: fixed started creating a stacking context
var browsers = {
    chrome: {
        fixed: 22
    }
};

// get browser version and name
// (we did not write this; if someone knows who did please let us know
// so we can attribute the code to the author!)
```

```
var browser = (function () {
    var N = navigator.appName;
    var ua = navigator.userAgent;
    var tem;
    var M = ua.match(
        /(opera|chrome|safari|firefox|msie)\/?\s*(\.?\d+(\.\d+)*)/i);
    if (M && (tem = ua.match(/version\/([\.\d]+)/i)) != null) {
        M[2] = tem[1];
    }
    M = M ? [M[1], M[2]] : [N, navigator.appVersion, '-?'];

    return {
        name: M[0].toLowerCase(),
        version: M[1]
    };
})();
```

The following functions are used to determine if an element creates a stacking context:

```
// use browser and version to determine if position: fixed
// creates a stacking context
var isFixedStackingCtx = (function () {
    return browsers[browser.name].fixed >= parseInt(browser.version, 10);
})();

// is a value a function?
function isFunction(thing) {
    return typeof thing === 'function';
}

// if element is positioned and has a z-index other than 0
// it creates a stacking context
function isPosAndHasZindex(el) {
    return el.style.position !== 'static' && el.style.zIndex !== 'auto';
}

// these values cause an element to create a stacking context
function doesStyleCreateStackingCtx(el) {
    var styles = el.style;

    if (styles.opacity < 1) {
        return true;
    }
    if (styles.transform !== 'none') {
        return true;
    }
    if (styles.transformStyle === 'preserve-3d') {
        return true;
    }
    if (styles.perspective !== 'none') {
        return true;
    }
```

```
    if (styles.flowFrom !== 'none' && styles.content !== 'normal') {
        return true;
    }
    if (styles.position === 'fixed' && isFixedStackingCtx) {
        return true;
    }

    return false;
}
```

Determining if an element creates a stacking context

The first thing our z-index manager needs to be able to do is determine if an element creates a stacking context. So, we need to translate the stacking context rules to code.

 All Jenga method code examples will omit other methods except the one currently being described. A completed Jenga object example will be provided later.

Our isStackingCtx function looks like this:

```
var jenga = {
    isStackingCtx: function (el) {
        return el.tagName === 'HTML' ||
            (isPosAndHasZindex(el) && doesStyleCreateStackingCtx(el));
    }
};
```

Finding an element's stacking context

We can now use the function from the previous section to find an element's stacking context. This information is useful for adjusting an element's z-index within a stacking context:

```
var jenga = {

    getStackingCtx: function (el) {
        var parentNode = el.parentNode;

        // recurse up the DOM tree until a stacking
        // context is found
        while (!jenga.isStackingCtx(parentNode)) {
            parentNode = parentNode.parentNode;
        }

        return parentNode;
```

```
        }
    };
```

Modifying an element's z-index

This is where things get interesting! This section will describe adjusting an element's z-index to move it to the top or bottom of a stacking context.

The first step is to create a function, moveUpDown, that will move an element to the top or bottom of the stack, creating a stacking context along the way if that is the desired behavior. The reason for creating a stacking context is that the element that is being moved to the top or the bottom may be part of another stacking context much further up the tree. If this is the case, then it is necessary to adjust the last ancestor of the element whose z-index is to be adjusted that is the first descendant of the current stacking context. This option is specified through the createStackingCtx argument, which can have either a Boolean or a function value. If it is a Boolean and the value is true, then it will create a stacking context by setting the element's parent's position to relative and setting the z-index to 0. If the value is a function, then it will be called and passed the element that should become a stacking context. It is then this function's responsibility to create a stacking context.

The moveUpDown function will also take three other parameters. The first is the element to move to the top or bottom, el. The next is the root element at which to stop adjusting z-indexes.

The root element argument is optional. It is useful for complex UI cases where there are several stacking contexts and simply raising the element in its direct stacking context may not bring it to the top because it could be nested in several other stacking contexts. One of the nested stacking contexts could cause the element to be hidden, because an ancestor could be toward the bottom of that context.

The last argument is increment. This accepts a Boolean value. true will send the element to the top of the stacking context and a falsy (*http://bit.ly/dwc-boolean*) value will send it to the bottom (back) stacking context.

The moveUpDown function looks like this:

```
function moveUpDown(el, createStackingCtx, root, increment) {
    var stackingCtxEl = jenga.getStackingCtx(el);

    // if element's parent node does not create a stacking context
    // and createStackingCtx is defined, then force a stacking
    // context to be created on the element's parent node
    if (createStackingCtx && stackingCtxEl !== el.parentNode) {
        // if developer provided a custom function for creating
        // a stacking context, then use it
        if (isFunction(createStackingCtx)) {
            createStackingCtx(el.parentNode);
```

```
        // create a stacking context in the least impactful
        // way to the DOM possible
        } else {
            el.parentNode.style.position = 'relative';
            el.parentNode.style.zIndex = 0;
        }
    }

    modifyZindex(el, increment); // defined in the next code block
    if (root && (root !== jenga.getStackingCtx(el) &&
        stackingCtxEl.tagName !== 'HTML')) {
        moveUpDown(stackingCtxEl, createStackingCtx, root, increment);
    }
}
```

Now for the really, really fun part! If you read the previous code block carefully, you probably noticed a reference to the modifyZindex function. This is where all the magic happens!

The modifyZindex function takes an element, finds the element that creates a stacking content, gets the child nodes of the stacking context, and then raises or lowers the z-index value of el until it is at the top or bottom of the stack:

```
function modifyZindex(el, increment) {
    var stackingCtxEl = jenga.getStackingCtx(el);
    var siblings = stackingCtxEl.childNodes;
    var siblingsMaxMinZindex = increment ? 0 : -1;

    var siblingZindex;

    // loop through element's siblings
    for (var i = 0; i < siblings.length; i++) {
        // if current element has a z-index and is not el...
        if (siblings[i].nodeType === 1 && isPosAndHasZindex(siblings[i]) &&
            siblings[i] !== el) {
            // check if sibling has a z-index value
            siblingZindex = parseInt(siblings[i].style.zIndex, 10);
            if (isNaN(siblingZindex)) {
                continue;
            }

            if (increment) {
                // update max z-index value for siblings
                siblingsMaxMinZindex = siblingZindex > siblingsMaxMinZindex ?
                    siblingZindex : siblingsMaxMinZindex;
            } else {
                // update min z-index value for siblings
                siblingsMaxMinZindex = siblingsMaxMinZindex < 0 ||
                    siblingZindex < siblingsMaxMinZindex ?
                    siblingZindex : siblingsMaxMinZindex;
            }
        }
    }
```

```
        }

        // if adjusted z-index is 0 and we're sending to the back, bump
        // all other elements up by 1
        if (!siblingsMaxMinZindex && !increment) {
            for (i = 0; i < siblings.length; i++) {
                if (siblings[i].nodeType === 1 && siblings[i] !== el) {
                    siblingZindex = parseInt(siblings[i].style.zIndex, 10);
                    if (isNaN(siblingZindex)) {
                        continue;
                    }

                    siblings[i].style.zIndex = ++siblingZindex;
                }
            }
        }

        // adjust element's z-index
        el.style.zIndex = increment ? siblingsMaxMinZindex + 1 :
            (siblingsMaxMinZindex ? siblingsMaxMinZindex - 1 : 0);
}
```

Now that we can determine an element's stacking context, we can bring it to the top of its stacking context:

```
// Bring an element to the top of stacking context
var jenga = {

    bringToFront: function (el, createStackingCtx, root) {
        moveUpDown(el, createStackingCtx, root, true);
    }

};
```

And now that we can send an element to the top of a stacking context, we can just as easily send it to the back by inverting the rules:

```
var jenga = {

    sendToBack: function (el, createStackingCtx, root) {
        moveUpDown(el, createStackingCtx, root, false);
    }
};
```

Example usages

Now that we have a fully functioning z-index manager, let's take a look at some example calls:

```
var el = document.getElementById('some-id');
var rootEl = document.getElementsByTagName('body')[0];
```

```
// bring an element to the top
// create stacking contexts
jenga.bringToFront(el, true);

// bring an element to the top
// do NOT create stacking contexts
jenga.bringToFront(el, false);

// bring an element to the top, including all ancestor stacking contexts
// create stacking contexts
jenga.bringToFront(el, true, rootEl);

// send an element to the back
// create stacking contexts
jenga.sendToBack(el, true);

// send an element to the back
// do NOT create stacking contexts
jenga.sendToBack(el, false);

// send an element to the back, including all ancestor stacking contexts
// create stacking contexts
jenga.sendToBack(el, true, rootEl);
```

Summary

We now have a nice API for determining stacking contexts and adjusting an element's z-index, ensuring that it is placed in the top rendering layer or the bottom rendering layer. This functionality is very useful when creating components where we need to ensure an element is on the top of a stack, such as a dialog or tooltip. It is also useful in complex applications in which stacking contexts and z-indexes frequently change. It ensures that the element in question will still render in the correct layer even if a z-index range guideline is not followed or a third-party plugin modifies the DOM.

Converting to a jQuery Plugin

As pervasive as jQuery is on the Web, it is sometimes a good idea to create a plugin wrapper for code in order to reach a larger audience. However, a plugin wrapper should only be created if the code provides a limited and specific set of functionality on an element or a collection of elements. The z-index manager is a good candidate because it is only concerned with adjusting z-indexes (limited and specific) on a single element or its ancestors (a collection of elements).

The jQuery website provides an excellent introductory tutorial (*http://bit.ly/dwc-jquery-tutorial*) for creating plugins. It covers the basic structure, chaining, options, etc.

Following is the code we use to create the plugin wrapper for our z-index manager:

```
// account for AMD
(function (factory) {
    if (typeof define === 'function' && define.amd) {
        define(['jquery'], factory);
    } else {
        factory(jQuery);
    }
}(function ($) {
    // Jenga code is here
    // https://github.com/jstrimpel/jenga/blob/master/dist/jenga.plugin.js

    $.fn.bringToFront = function (options) {
        options = options || {};
        if (this[0]) {
            jenga.bringToFront(this[0], options.createStackingCtx, options.root);
        }
        return this;
    };

    $.fn.sendToBack = function (options) {
        options = options || {};
        if (this[0]) {
            jenga.sendToBack(this[0], options.createStackingCtx, options.root);
        }
        return this;
    };

    $.fn.isStackingCtx = function () {
        return this[0] ? jenga.isStackingCtx(this[0]) : false;
    };

    $.fn.getStackingCtx = function () {
        return this[0] ? jenga.getStackingCtx(this[0]) : undefined;
    };

}));
```

Vanilla JavaScript and native DOM APIs were used for the z-index manager, as opposed to leveraging jQuery. This was done for a few different reasons. First, native DOM APIs are faster than jQuery, and speed is of the essence when code impacts rendering. Second, there was not much to gain by leveraging jQuery—there were no browser quirks to abstract, nor was there a need to encapsulate or simplify native APIs. Lastly, plugin wrapper aside, I completely removed the dependency on jQuery. As difficult as it is to imagine, some people do not use jQuery (an alternative is AngularJS (*http://angularjs.org*)). I am not opposed to using jQuery—I actually advocate its usage. However, I believe that developers should always weigh the pros and cons of adding a dependency to a project, and in this case the pros did not outweigh the cons of including jQuery as a dependency.

Adding z-index Management to the Dialog Widget

We will now be applying the information from this chapter to our dialog widget. If you remember, the dialog widget had a show method. This method should show the dialog and bring it to the top of the stack:

```
Dialog.prototype.show = function () {
    jenga.bringToFront(this.$el[0]);
};
```

This example strictly shows the application of the code from this chapter to a specific method of the dialog widget. Other details, such as positioning the dialog and packaging, will be covered in later chapters. However, if you absolutely, positively cannot wait, the completed dialog example from Part I can be viewed on GitHub (*https://github.com/webcomponentsbook*).

Summary

In this chapter we took a deep dive into the layering of elements on the z-axis. We discovered why the seemingly simple z-index property baffles even the seasoned frontend engineer. We gained an understanding of stacking order rules, stacking contexts, and how changing the values of certain element properties can greatly impact the layering of an element on a web page. Armed with this information, we explored why simply increasing or decreasing the z-index value of an element does not necessarily have the outcome one would expect. We then formulated a strategy for properly managing the layering of elements in a web application by classifying and assigning z-index ranges for UI elements. Next, we looked at a programmatic approach for layering elements in nondeterministic UIs, creating a library, Jenga, that we can use to manage the layering of elements in any application. We looked briefly at how to create a jQuery plugin for our code, and finally, we incorporated the Jenga library into the dialog widget.

Building Our UI

The Dialog Widget

In Part II, we will continue constructing the dialog widget introduced in Part I. If you skipped the first part of the book and would like to learn about the design and implementation details of the dialog widget, please refer back to Chapter 2. Subsequent chapters in Part I contain sections that apply the concepts they cover to the dialog widget as well. These sections are located toward the ends of the chapters and can be referenced as needed for understanding code in the dialog widget not introduced in Part II.

Part II introduces concepts and patterns that are typically abstracted away from day-to-day frontend development by libraries such as Dojo (*http://dojotoolkit.org*), jQuery UI (*http://jqueryui.com*), Kendo UI (*http://www.kendoui.com*), and Twitter Bootstrap (*http://getbootstrap.com*). These concepts and patterns are used to implement UI widgets that you probably work with on a daily basis as a frontend engineer. After reading this part of the book, you will have a solid understanding of how elements are positioned and how to manipulate element positions using JavaScript.

 If you skipped Chapter 2, you might find yourself asking, "Why are we building a widget? I thought this was a web components book!" That's a valid question. The answer is that this book is more than just a rehashing of the Web Components specification. It is designed to provide a better understanding of the DOM by exploring the details underlying today's widget interfaces. Knowledge of these details is required to build moderately complex web components, and what better way to understand these details than through a concrete example?

Cloning Nodes

Jason Strimpel

Frequently when you see a drag-and-drop interface on the Web, nodes are being cloned—that is, copies of the original nodes are being made (using the `cloneNode` method, described in the next section). This is done because it is more efficient to clone the node that is being dragged than it would be to detach it from its original location in the DOM, reattach it, and then move it. This is especially true in the case where a user tries to drop the node outside of the defined drop target—the cloned node is deleted and the original node is then shown again, without having to be detached and reattached. If the cloned node is successfully dropped into the target node, then it remains, and the original node is deleted. Cloning can also be useful in the case where you do not want the original node to be removed or hidden until the cloned node is dropped into a target.

Another use case in which cloning is useful is for copying nodes. For instance, an interface may need to provide the functionality for classifying items by one or more characteristics. This functionality could be accomplished by creating an interface that allows a user to drop items into different drop targets, which could be easily accomplished by cloning nodes.

A third use case is that you want to perform some calculations based on a node's dimensions. For instance, if the node contains text of an unknown length that needs to be truncated in a unique fashion—e.g., the beginning and end of the text need to remain, but an undetermined amount needs to be trimmed from the middle—then the containing node can be cloned and the necessary measurements can be done in a rendering layer below the default rendering layer, out of view. Once the string has been truncated accordingly, it can be inserted into the original node, and the clone can then be deleted.

Cloning nodes incurs overhead and is not always the best approach. Cases where a simple click event or form value change moves a node to another location in the DOM are not good cloning candidates, because these types of actions are not subject to the error that can occur when a human is manually moving nodes.

Using the cloneNode Method

All browsers natively support cloning nodes via a node's `cloneNode` (*https://devel oper.mozilla.org/en-US/docs/Web/API/Node.cloneNode*) method. The method accepts an optional argument for creating a *deep clone*, which clones all descendant nodes:

```
var el = document.querySelector('.some-class');

// shallow clone
var elShallowClone = el.cloneNode(false);

// deep clone
var elDeepClone = el.cloneNode(true);
```

 The default value for `cloneNode`'s deep argument has changed between browser versions as the specification has changed. The current default value is `false`. To ensure backward compatibility, always pass the deep argument.

When a node is cloned, all of its attributes and values are copied to the clone. This includes inline listeners, but it does not include any event listeners bound using `addEventListener` (*http://bit.ly/dwc-addevent*) or those assigned to element properties:

```
<!-- inline event handler -->
<!-- this will be bound to the cloned node -->
<div onclick="someFunction();">Click Me</dv>

var el = document.querySelector('.some-class');

// addListener; this will not be bound to the cloned node
el.addEventListener('click', function (e) {
    // someone clicked me
}, false);

// bound using element property; this will not be bound to the cloned node
el.onclick = function (e) {
    // someone clicked me again
};
```

cloneNode does not attach the returned node to the document. The node can be attached to the document using appendChild (*http://bit.ly/dwc-appendchild*) or a similar method for adding a node to the document:

```
var elToClone = document.querySelector('.clone-me-please');
var elToAppend = elToClone.cloneNode(true); // ***not part of the DOM***

// add cloned node to the DOM
document.body.appendChild.appendChild(elCloneToAppend);
```

cloneNode copies all attributes and properties, so be careful not to create duplicate element IDs when cloning nodes. Duplicate IDs are technically not allowed because they are supposed to be unique identifiers, but in practice browsers do allow them. Having duplicate IDs can cause problems when code is expecting only a single element to be returned when querying for an element by ID.

Using jQuery.clone

The native cloneNode method works well for cloning nodes and their attributes, but it does not do a good job of cloning events bound to the element being cloned. Fortunately, jQuery has a method, $.clone (*http://api.jquery.com/clone/*), for ensuring that all events bound by jQuery can be copied to the new element if this is the desired behavior. This means that any events bound by $.on, $.bind, $.click, etc. are copied if the withDataAndEvents or deepWithDataAndEvents argument is set to true.

$.clone always does a deep clone (i.e., clones all descendant nodes of the nodes matched by the query selector passed to $), so use caution when cloning. Otherwise, you could end up copying very large branches of the DOM tree, which could be a very costly operation.

The $.clone method is used as follows:

```
var $el = $('.clone-me-please');

// clone without data and events
var $clone1 = $el.clone(false);

// clone with data and events for $el and all children
var $clone2 = $el.clone(true);

// deep clone with data and events for only $el
var $clone3 = $el.clone(true, false);
```

jQuery is able to copy the events because it keeps an internal cache of all event handlers it binds. This is also what enables it to automatically remove event handlers when elements are explicitly removed ($.remove) or implicitly removed ($.html). This is done to help prevent any references to elements that have been removed from the DOM from being retained, which helps reduce memory leaks.

 $.clone does not copy event handlers bound to an element outside of jQuery unless they are inline event handlers (e.g., <div onclick="someFunction();">).

In addition to copying all event handlers bound by jQuery, jQuery.clone also copies all data that was related to an element via $.data.

 Arrays and objects are copied by reference, not by value, so all cloned nodes' data as well as the original node's data will point to the same arrays and objects. A shallow copy of an array or object can be done after the node is cloned, as seen in the following code examples.

You use the $.data and $.clone methods as follows:

```
// get a reference to a jQuery selection and set data
// on the element
var $el = $('.some-el');
$el.data({
    arr: [1,2,3],
    obj: { foo: 'bar' }
});

// get references to the data from the elements
var arr = $el.data('arr');
var obj = $el.data('obj');

// jQuery provides a utility method for copying arrays and objects
var arrCopy = $.extend([], arr);
var objCopy = $.extend({}, obj);

// clone $el and set copies
$clone = $el.clone(true);
$clone.data({
    arr: arrCopy,
    obj: objCopy
});

// if someone ever asks you how to copy an array or object in an interview...
var arrCopy = arr.slice(0);

var objCopy = {};
for (var k in obj) {
```

```
        objCopy[k] = obj[k];
    }

    // then say whoomp, there it is!
    // if they are past a certain age they will appreciate this reference
    // and your poor sense of humor :)
```

Continuation of the Dialog Widget

Oftentimes, a widget gets a reference to a DOM element. This element is then used as the container for the widget. In other cases the element is cloned because the original element should not be modified. The dialog will be treated as the latter case because its containing element will be appended to the <body>. This makes managing the z-index much easier, because it will only be competing with other elements that are children of the <body>. Additionally, the dialog widget should not make any assumptions as to the consumer's alternate intended uses of that element. It could be used for other purposes than just the dialog widget, and if it were used directly any modifications made to the element by the dialog widget could inadvertently impact other areas of the web application. For these reasons, the dialog widget will do a deep clone of the element passed during construction using $.clone if options.clone is true (this option enables developers to decide whether or not to clone, providing them with a convenient API for avoiding the aforementioned issues):

```
function Dialog (options) {
    // optionally clone dialog $el
    options.$el = options.clone ? $(options.$el).clone() :
        $(options.$el);
    // append to body
    if (options.appendToEl) {
        $(options.appendToEl).append(options.$el);
    }

    Voltron.call(this, options);

    return this;
}
```

Summary

In this chapter we introduced the concept of cloning nodes and presented some common use cases. We then covered the native method for cloning nodes, cloneNode, and the jQuery method, jQuery.clone. We discussed the enhanced event handler copying provided by the jQuery.clone method, then took this knowledge and applied it to the dialog widget as an illustration of how to handle cases in which the node selected to create a widget should be copied and not used to directly to create the widget instance.

You now have the proper background information to clone nodes effectively in any situation, and a working example. For more information on cloning nodes please refer to the MDN cloneNode documentation (*http://bit.ly/dwc-clonenode*) and the jQuery.clone documentation (*http://api.jquery.com/clone/*).

Constructing an Overlay

Jason Strimpel

Anytime you see a tooltip, dialog, drop-down menu, etc. on the Web, an *overlay* is likely driving the component. This is especially likely if reusability was a design concern or if the requirements called for more than CSS alone could provide.

An overlay is a widget that provides basic functionality for positioning an element relative to the document or another element. You can think of an overlay as a new window that is part of the document. It is an element in the DOM: a blank canvas that can contain any content that you want. This lower-level widget can then be extended, mixed in, or applied to another widget to create a widget with which a user interacts (such as our dialog widget).

An overlay should have two primary functions. First, it should be able to position an element relative to the viewport. This is useful for directing a user's focus to a critical item such as an error. Second, the overlay should be able to position an element relative to another element in the document. This functionality allows a developer to bring attention to a specific item on the page—e.g., a tooltip—or position related items, such as a drop-down for constructing UI controls.

This chapter will discuss how to construct an overlay. This overlay will be used to add more functionality to the dialog widget.

Defining an API

Before getting into the details of the overlay code, let's stub out an API to help us determine the necessary supporting private methods and where we can gain reuse across the public API methods. Our overlay library will be called Duvet:

```
// pass in dependencies to closure - window, jQuery, and z-index manager
var Duvet = (function (global, $, jenga) {
```

```
'use strict';

// default options
var defaults = {
    alignToEl: null,
    align: 'M',
    fixed: true,
    offsets: {
        top: 0,
        right: 0,
        bottom: 0,
        left: 0
    }
};

// creates an overlay instance
function Duvet(el, options) {
    // create references to overlay element
    this.el = el;
    this.$el = $(el);

    // extend default options with developer-defined options
    this.setOptions(options);

    // return instance reference
    return this;
}

// positions the overlay element
Duvet.prototype.position = function (options) {};

// sets instance options
Duvet.prototype.setOptions = function (options) {};

// clears out any developer-defined references to ensure
// that no element references remain - i.e., helps prevent
// memory leaks!
Duvet.prototype.destroy = function (options) {};

return Duvet;

})(window, jQuery, jenga);
```

 There is a great deal of functionality that can be added to an overlay widget. The overlay in this chapter is intentionally simple and meant to be a starting point for understanding how an overlay works.

Utilities

There are some utility methods and functions that can be defined within the overlay widget's closure. These are introduced in the following sections.

 These methods could potentially be moved to a component utility library to be shared across all components that need to perform calculations for sizing and positioning elements.

Detecting Scrollbar Width

When positioning an element, it is sometimes necessary to account for the width of the containing element's scrollbar. The space the scrollbar occupies is not automatically subtracted from an element's `offsetWidth` and `offsetHeight`, and this space needs to be accounted for so that the overlay can be positioned precisely. You can get the width of an element's scrollbar with the following function:

```
function getScrollbarWidth(parentEl) {
    var innerCss = {
        width: '100%',
        height: '200px'
    };
    var outerCss = {
        width: '200px',
        // outer element height is smaller than inner element height;
        // this will cause a scrollbar
        height: '150px',
        position: 'absolute',
        top: 0,
        left: 0,
        visibility: 'hidden',
        overflow: 'hidden'
    };
    var $inner = $('<div>test</div>').css(innerCss);
    var $outer = $('<div></div>').css(outerCss).append($inner);
    var innerEl = $inner[0];
    var outerEl = $outer[0];

    $(parentEl || 'body').append(outerEl);
    // get the layout width of the inner element, including the scrollbar
    var innerWidth = innerEl.offsetWidth;
    $outer.css('overflow', 'scroll');
    // get the inner width of the outer element, NOT including the scrollbar
    var outerWidth = $outer[0].clientWidth;
    // remove the elements from the DOM
    $outer.remove();

    // subtract the outer element width from the inner element width -
```

```
    // this difference is the width of the scrollbar
    return (innerWidth - outerWidth);
}

// cache value for cases where scrollbar widths are consistent
var scrollbarWidth = getScrollbarWidth();
```

 If there is a possibility that containing elements will have differing scrollbar widths, then getScrollbarWidth needs to be executed each time an overlay is instantiated and the value saved as a property of that instance. The containing element's calculated property for the scrollbar width will have to be applied to the element against which the measurement is being done. Duvet will assume the worst-case scenario and execute getScrollbarWidth every time it positions an element.

Accounting for the Scrollbar When Calculating a Containing Element's Width

Once the scrollbar width for an element has been determined, it can be used to determine the actual amount of available space in the containing element. This can be done by subtracting the containing element's scrollWidth and scrollHeight from the element's offsetWidth and offsetHeight, respectively, enabling you to calculate the proper position for the overlay:

```
// scrollWidth and scrollHeight values will be larger than the actual
// width or height of the element itself if the content exceeds the
// width or height; in this case, the scrollbar width needs to be
// accounted for when positioning the overlay element
function getScrollbarOffset(el) {
    var $el = $(el);
    var $body = $('body');
    var scrollWidth = el.scrollWidth === undefined ? $body[0].scrollWidth :
        el.scrollWidth;
    var scrollHeight = el.scrollHeight === undefined ? $body[0].scrollHeight :
        el.scrollHeight;
    var scrollbarWidth = getScrollbarWidth();

    return {
        x: scrollWidth > $el.outerWidth() ? scrollbarWidth : 0,
        y: scrollHeight > $el.outerHeight() ? scrollbarWidth : 0
    };
}
```

Getting an Element's Dimensions and Coordinates

The positioning of an overlay is done by using the overlay's dimensions and coordinates relative to the containing or aligning element's dimensions and coordinates. The overlay is then positioned absolutely relative to the containing element or the aligning element.

 An *aligning element* is an element next to which an overlay is positioned; e.g., an element over which a user hovers and a tooltip (overlay) is displayed.

We can use this function to get the dimensions of an element:

```
function getDimensions(el) {
    // https://developer.mozilla.org/en-US
    //     /docs/Web/API/Element.getBoundingClientRect
    // relative to the viewport
    var rect;
    // https://api.jquery.com/position/
    // relative to the offset parent
    var offset = el === window ? { top: 0, left: 0 } : $(el).position();

    // if containing element is the window object
    // then use $ methods for getting the width and height
    if (el === window) {
        var width = $(window).width();
        var height = $(window).height();

        rect = {
            right: width,
            left: 0,
            top: 0,
            bottom: height
        };
    } else {
        rect = el.getBoundingClientRect();
    }

    return {
        width: rect.right - rect.left,
        height: rect.bottom - rect.top,
        // top relative to the element's offset parent
        top: offset.top,
        // bottom relative to the element's offset parent
        bottom: offset.top + (rect.bottom - rect.top),
        // left relative to the element's offset parent
        left: offset.left,
        right: rect.right
```

```
    };
}
```

Listening for Resize and Scrolling Events

When an overlay is in a fixed position it should not move from its position relative to its containing element when the containing element has an overflow and is scrolled, or when the document window is resized. In order to maintain the fixed position, the overflow must reposition itself as the containing element is scrolled or resized.

 "Fixed position" in this case refers to the element being visually fixed, not having a `position` value of `fixed`.

Listeners are bound by passing a callback that adjusts the overlay element position to event handlers that listen for scroll and resize events:

```
function bindListeners($offsetParent, callback) {
    // unbind event to ensure that event listener is never bound more than once
    $offsetParent.off('scroll.duvet').on('scroll.duvet', function (e) {
        callback();
    });
    $offsetParent.off('resize.duvet').on('resize.duvet', function (e) {
        callback();
    });
}
```

Updating Options

An overlay's functionality may need to change at runtime. For instance, if it is being used to create a tooltip component, then you might not want to incur the overhead of setup and teardown every time the tooltip is triggered to be shown. This could be costly, because in each case an element would have to be created and destroyed. This could happen frequently if, for example, the user were hovering over a table containing cells that trigger tooltips to reveal additional information related to the cells' content. In the case of tooltips, it's much more efficient to have a function that can be used to reset the `el` and `alignTo` properties. Fortunately, there is just such a function:

```
Duvet.prototype.setOptions = function (options) {
    this.options = options ? $.extend(this.options, options) : this.options;
};
```

Destroying

A good practice for widget cleanup is to leave the DOM as you found it. The `destroy` function will simply null out the `el` and `alignTo` properties and unbind any event handlers to prevent potential memory leaks. The responsibility for the actual destruction of these elements lies outside the scope of the overlay widget, as it only applies a limited set of functionality to an element and should not make any assumptions as to the state of the element outside of its scope.

We use the `destroy` function as follows:

```
Duvet.prototype.destroy = function (options) {
    var $parent = $(el.parentNode);

    // unbind event handlers
    $parent.off('scroll.duvet');
    $parent.off('resize.duvet');

    // null out references
    this.el = null;
    this.$el = null;

    // clear out any developer-defined options
    this.options = defaults;
};
```

Positioning

When `<instance>.position` is called it will position the element using one of two private functions, defined in "JavaScript overlay" on page 65. `align` will be called if an element is to be aligned relative to another element. `position` will called if an element is to be positioned absolutely relative to its `offsetParent`:

```
Duvet.prototype.position = function (options) {
    // allow modification of options before positioning
    this.setOptions(options);

    // call private functions (will be defined later)
    if (this.options.alignToEl) {
        // if alignToEl is body, then reassign to window since body height
        // is equal to content height
        this.options.alignToEl = this.options.alignToEl.tagName === 'BODY' ?
            $(window)[0] : this.options.alignToEl;
        align(this.el, this.options);
    } else {
        position(this.el, this.options);
    }
};
```

Positioning an Element Relative to the Viewport or Another Element

There are a few different ways to position an element relative to the viewport or another element, depending upon the requirements. The simplest cases (e.g., where the element is centered and its position is fixed) can be handled with CSS alone, while more complicated examples, such as positioning an element that is draggable, require performing calculations based on the element's position relative to the viewport. Some of the code used to support this will be used to position an element relative to another element as well. The first method will be shown for informational purposes, but the latter method will be used in all other examples since it is more applicable to our working example—creating a dialog that could be draggable, but that has to be positioned absolutely. That said, there is no reason that the CSS example could not be incorporated into an overlay widget as an optimization.

CSS overlay

The following example (from "Fixed positioning" on page 28) shows how to create a simple centered overlay using only CSS:

```
/*
Covers the viewport when applied to an
element that is a child of the <body>.
It stretches the element across the <body> by
fixing its position and setting all the position
properties to 0. This makes it impossible to
interact with any elements that are in lower rendering
layers.
*/
.modal-overlay {
    position: fixed;
    top: 0;
    left: 0;
    right: 0;
    bottom: 0;
    background: #000;
    opacity: .5;
}

/*
Centers an element in the viewport by setting the top and left
properties to 50%. It then accounts for the height and width of the element
by taking half the height and width, and sets the top and left properties
respectively by negating these values.
*/
.modal-content {
    position: fixed;
    top:50%;
    left:50%;
    margin-top: -100px;
    margin-left: -200px;
```

```
    width: 400px;
    height: 200px;
    background: #fff;
    padding: 10px;
    overflow: auto;
}
<div class="modal-overlay"></div>
<div class="modal-content">I am the modal content. Fear me.</div>
```

JavaScript overlay

The next example shows how to create an overlay that is positioned relative to the
viewport or another element using JavaScript. This is useful for overlays that start out
centered, but can be dragged or moved about in the document:

```
function position(el, options) {
    var pos = {};
    var $parent = el.parentNode.tagName === 'BODY' ? $(window) : $(el.parentNode);
    var $el = $(el);
    // get the scrollbar offset
    var scrollbarOffset = getScrollbarOffset(el.parentNode.tagName === 'BODY' ?
        window : el.parentNode);

    //  parent el is the offset parent
    if (el.parentNode !== el.offsetParent) {
        el.parentNode.style.position = 'relative';
    }

    switch (options.align) {
        case 'TL':
            pos.top = 0;
            pos.left = 0;
            break;
        case 'TR':
            pos.top = 0;
            pos.right = 0;
            break;
        case 'BL':
            pos.bottom = 0;
            pos.left = 0;
            break;
        case 'BR':
            pos.bottom = 0;
            pos.right = 0;
            break;
        case 'BC':
            pos.bottom = 0;
            pos.left = ((($parent.outerWidth() -
                scrollbarOffset.y - $el.outerWidth()) / 2) +
                $parent.scrollLeft());
            break;
        case 'TC':
```

```
            pos.top = 0;
            break;
        case 'M':
            pos.left = ((($parent.outerWidth() -
                scrollbarOffset.y - $el.outerWidth()) / 2) +
                $parent.scrollLeft());
            pos.top = ((($parent.outerHeight() -
                scrollbarOffset.x - $el.outerHeight()) / 2) +
                $parent.scrollTop());
            break;
    }

    // if the positions are less than 0 then the
    // element being positioned is larger than
    // its container
    pos.left = pos.left > 0 ? pos.left : 0;
    pos.top = pos.top > 0 ? pos.top : 0;

    // position the element absolutely and
    // set the top and left properties
    $el.css($.extend({
        position: 'absolute',
        display: 'block'
    }, pos));

    // if the element should not move when the containing
    // element is resized or scrolled then bind event listeners
    // and call the position function
    if (options.fixed && options.align === 'M' && !options.bound) {
        options.bound = true;
        bindListeners($parent, function () {
            position(el, options);
        });
    }
}
```

Positioning an Element Relative to Another Element

It is often useful to position an element relative to another element. Common use cases include tooltips, drop-downs, and UI controls (sliders). These types of use cases require the ability to define different positions, such as top center, bottom right, middle, bottom left, etc.

The following functions can be used to position one element relative to another:

```
// used to get the margins for offset parents
function getMargins(el) {
    var $el = $(el);
    var marginTop = parseInt($el.css('margin-top'), 10);
    var marginLeft = parseInt($el.css('margin-left'), 10);
```

```
    return {
        top: isNaN(marginTop) ? 0 : marginTop,
        left: isNaN(marginLeft) ? 0 : marginLeft
    };
}

// align the overlay el to another element in the DOM
function align(el, options) {
    var alignToElDim = getDimensions(options.alignToEl);
    var css = { display: 'block', visibility: 'visible', position: 'absolute' };
    var $el = $(el);
    var parentAlignToElMargins = getMargins(options.alignToEl.parentNode);

    // hide element, but keep dimensions by setting the visibility to hidden
    $el.css({
        visibility: 'hidden',
        display: 'block',
        'z-index': -1000
    });

    // get element's dimensions
    var elDim = getDimensions(el);

    // ensure that alignToEl parent el is the offset parent
    if (options.alignToEl.parentNode !== options.alignToEl.offsetParent) {
        options.alignToEl.parentNode.style.position = 'relative';
    }

    // use the alignToEl and el dimensions and positions to calculate
    // the el's position
    switch (options.align) {
        case 'TL':
            css.top = (alignToElDim.top - elDim.height) -
                parentAlignToElMargins.top;
            css.left = alignToElDim.left - parentAlignToElMargins.left;
            break;
        case 'TR':
            css.top = (alignToElDim.top - elDim.height) -
                parentAlignToElMargins.top;
            css.left = (alignToElDim.right - elDim.width)  -
                parentAlignToElMargins.left;
            break;
        case 'BL':
            css.top = alignToElDim.bottom  - parentAlignToElMargins.top;
            css.left = alignToElDim.left - parentAlignToElMargins.left;
            break;
        case 'BR':
            css.top = alignToElDim.bottom - parentAlignToElMargins.top;
            css.left = (alignToElDim.right - elDim.width) -
                parentAlignToElMargins.left;
            break;
```

```
            case 'BC':
                css.top = alignToElDim.bottom - parentAlignToElMargins.top;
                css.left = (((alignToElDim.width - elDim.width) / 2) +
                    alignToElDim.left) - parentAlignToElMargins.left;
                break;
            case 'TC':
                css.top = (alignToElDim.top - elDim.height) -
                    parentAlignToElMargins.top;
                css.left = (((alignToElDim.width - elDim.width) / 2) +
                    alignToElDim.left) - parentAlignToElMargins.left;
                break;
            case 'M':
                css.top = (((alignToElDim.height - elDim.height) / 2) +
                    alignToElDim.top) - parentAlignToElMargins.top;
                css.left = (((alignToElDim.width - elDim.width) / 2) +
                    alignToElDim.left) - parentAlignToElMargins.left;
                break;
        }

    jenga.bringToFront(el, true);
    $el.css(css);
}
```

Adding the Overlay to the Dialog Widget

In the previous chapter we added z-index management to the dialog widget. Since
Jenga, the z-index manager, is now a dependency of the overlay library, the call to
Jenga can be completely replaced by a call to the overlay library:

```
function Dialog (options) {
    // optionally clone dialog $el
    options.$el = options.clone ? $(options.$el).clone() :
        $(options.$el);
    // append to body
    if (options.appendToEl) {
        $(options.appendToEl).append(options.$el);
    }

    Voltron.call(this, options);
    // create overlay instance

    this.overlay = new Duvet(this.$el[0]);
    return this;
}

Dialog.prototype.show = function () {
    // this will adjust z-index, set the display property,
    // and position the dialog
    this.overlay.position();
};
```

```
Dialog.prototype.destroy = function () {
    // clean up overlay
    this.overlay.destroy();

    // call superclass
    Voltron.prototype.destroy.call(this);
};
```

Summary

In this chapter we constructed a fully functioning overlay. In order to accomplish that, we first created utility methods to measure and account for scrollbars, and to get the dimensions of an element. Next, we covered resize and scroll event listeners for overlays that are fixed in a container—either an element or the document's <body>. Then we covered both CSS and JavaScript techniques for positioning and aligning an element. Finally, we applied this knowledge to the dialog widget.

Making Elements Draggable

Frequently in web applications you will see elements that are draggable—slider handles, dialogs, column resizing handles, etc. If you have ever wondered exactly how this is accomplished, or needed to implement this behavior, then this is the chapter for you! The first step in the process is learning about mouse events.

 This and subsequent chapters will utilize *jQuery events*, which, for the most part, are wrappers to native JavaScript events that are normalized for cross-browser consistency.

Mouse Events

jQuery supports eleven different mouse events (*http://api.jquery.com/category/events/mouse-events/*). However, making an element draggable only requires understanding three of these events: `$.mousemove`, `$.mousedown`, and `$.mouseup`.

$.mousemove

Tracking mouse movements is fundamental to making an element draggable because the mouse position will be used to coordinate the movement of the element being dragged. The native JavaScript `mousemove` event provides the mouse position data, such as the values of `clientX` and `clientY`, which are properties of the native event object. However, support for these properties varies between browsers. Fortunately, jQuery normalizes these properties as part of the jQuery event object. We bind the `$.mousemove` event listener as follows:

```
$('body').on('mousemove', function (e) {
    // log the normalized mouse coordinates
    console.log('pageX: ' + e.pageX + ' ' + 'pageY: ' + e.pageY);
});
```

 mousemove is useful for tracking user mouse movements, which can be used to gather analytics. These analytics can be used to improve the functionality of a UI by helping users to get to information and complete frequent actions faster.

$.mousedown

Determining when a user presses the mouse button (mousedown (*http://api.jquery.com/mousedown/*) event) is required for dragging elements because this is the event that marks the moment when the mousemove event translates into moving the element marked to be dragged. We bind the $.mousedown event listener as follows:

```
$('body').on('mousedown', function (e) {
    console.log('Yo. You just pressed the mouse down.');
});
```

$.mouseup

Knowing when to stop moving an element is the final step during a drag sequence. As soon as the mouseup (*http://api.jquery.com/mouseup/*) event is fired, the last mouse position is used to determine the final location of the element being dragged. We bind this event listener as follows:

```
$('body').on('mouseup', function (e) {
    console.log('Dude. You just let the mouse go up.');
});
```

Mouse Events Best Practices

In addition to knowing the required mouse events for making an element draggable, it is equally important to know how to optimize the usage of these events. I do not advocate premature optimization, but these are not strictly optimizations: they are common patterns and best practices that have been vetted by UI widget libraries such as jQuery UI. jQuery advocates their usage as well.

1. Bind $.mousemove on $.mousedown

mousemove is triggered every time the mouse is moved, even if it is only by a pixel. This means hundreds of events can easily be triggered in a matter of seconds if a user is interacting with a UI that requires frequent mouse movements. To ensure that mousemove events are only processed when necessary, it is best to bind the $.mousemove handler on $.mousedown:

```
$('.some-element').on('mousedown', function (e) {
    $('.some-element').on('mousemove', function (e) {
        // this is where the dragging magic will happen
    });
});
```

2. Unbind $.mousemove on $.mouseup

Just as you should only bind the $.mousemove handler on $.mousedown, you should *unbind* the $.mousemove handler on $.mouseup—for every action. This will prevent any unnecessary mousemove events from being processed after the dragging of the element has been completed:

```
$('body').on('mouseup', function (e) {
    // stop processing mousemove events
    $('.some-element').off('mousemove');
});
```

3. Bind $.mouseup to the <body>

You may have noticed in the previous code block that the mouseup event was bound to the <body>. This is because, according to the API documentation (*http://api.jquery.com/mousemove/*), in some cases "the mouseup event might be sent to a different HTML element than the mousemove event was." For this reason alone, it is best to always bind the $.mouseup handler to the <body> tag.

4. Namespace All Event Bindings

It is always a good practice to namespace (*http://api.jquery.com/event.namespace/*) all event bindings. This ensures that events that are bound by a widget do not conflict with other event handlers, which makes cleanup easier as you don't have to worry about destroying event handlers bound by processes outside of the widget. Since the $.mouseup event handler is bound to the <body>, the namespace is also used to filter out other mouse events that have bubbled up to the <body>:

```
// namespace all events
$('body').on('mouseup.draggable', function (e) {

});
```

Defining an API

In order to make our code for making an element draggable more reusable, it is necessary to create an object with a convenient API that can be applied to any element:

```
// I can move any mountain
var Shamen = (function (global, $) {

    'use strict';

    // instance default options
    var defaults = {
        dragHandle: null
    };

    // create draggable instance
    function Shamen(el, options) {
        this.options = $.extend({}, defaults, options);
        var css = { cursor: (this.options.cursor || 'move') };

        // check if element is a child of a document fragment (i.e.,
        // a shadow DOM); this will be important later
        this.isChildOfDocFragment = isChildOfDocFragment(el);
        this.el = el;
        this.$el = $(el);
        this.$dragHandle = this.options.dragHandle ?
            this.$el.find(this.options.dragHandle) : this.$el;
        this.bind();
        this.originalDragHandleCursor = this.$dragHandle.css('cursor');
        // apply cursor css
        this.$dragHandle.css(css);
    }

    // bind mousedown event handler
    Shamen.prototype.bind = function () {

    };

    // clean up to prevent memory leaks
    Shamen.prototype.destroy = function () {

    };

    return Shamen;

})(window, jQuery);
```

Creating a Drag Handle

In some cases you only want a specific child element of the draggable element to be the drag handle, as opposed to the entire element. For instance, in the case of a dialog it is often the title or header bar that is the drag handle.

 A drag handle is an element that responds to a drag or resize event when a `mousedown` event occurs, allowing a user to move or resize an ancestor node of the drag handle. In this book the ancestor element will be the widget's `el` or `$el` property.

We can implement a drag handle as follows:

```
.drag-handle {
    cursor: move;
}
<div class="draggable">
    <div class="drag-handle"></div>
</div>

$('.draggable').on('mousedown.draggable', '.drag-handle', function (e) {

});
```

Making Things Move

Now that the nuts and bolts of making an element draggable have been defined, it is time to use these pieces to make something move!

$.mousedown Handler

The first step is to write the `$.mousedown` handler, which gets the mouse's current position:

```
// bind mousedown event handler
Shamen.prototype.bind = function () {
    // filter on drag handle if developer defined one
    var selector = this.options.dragHandle || null;
    var self = this;
    // account for margins if element is position absolutely;
    // code reused from Duvet.js
    var parentMargins = this.$el.attr('position') === 'absolute' ?
        getMargins(this.$el.parent()[0]) : { top: 0, left: 0};;

    this.$el.on('mousedown.shamen', selector, function (e) {
        // get the initial mouse position
        var mousePos = {
            x: e.pageX,
```

```
            y: e.pageY
        };
    });
};
```

$.mousemove Handler

This is where the moving of an element occurs! On mousemove the $.mousemove handler uses the element dimension and position values set in the $.mousedown handler to move the draggable element pixel for pixel as mousemove events are triggered:

```
// bind mousedown event handler
Shamen.prototype.bind = function () {
    // filter on drag handle if developer defined one
    var selector = this.options.dragHandle || null;
    var self = this;
    // account for margins if element is position absolutely;
    // code reused from Duvet.js
    var parentMargins = this.$el.attr('position') === 'absolute' ?
        getMargins(this.$el.parent()[0]) : { top: 0, left: 0};

    this.$el.on('mousedown.shamen', selector, function (e) {
        // get the initial mouse position
        var mousePos = {
            x: e.pageX,
            y: e.pageY
        };

        // bind mousemove event handler
        $(window).on('mousemove.shamen', function (e) {
            // get the differences between the mousedown position and the
            // positions from the mousemove events
            var xDiff = e.pageX - mousePos.x;
            var yDiff = e.pageY - mousePos.y;
            // get the draggable el's current position relative to the document
            var elPos = {
                left: el.offsetLeft,
                top: el.offsetTop
            };

            // apply the mouse position differences to the el's position
            self.$el.css({
                top: elPos.top + yDiff,
                left: elPos.left + xDiff
            });

            // store the current mouse position
            // to diff with the next mousemove positions
            mousePos = {
                x: e.pageX,
                y: e.pageY
            };
```

```
    });
  });
};
```

$.mouseup Handler

When the mouseup event is fired the $.mousemove handler is unbound, and the drag-gable element is in its final resting place (at least, until dragging is initiated again by another mousedown event). The $.mouseup event handler looks like this:

```
// bind mousedown event handler
Shamen.prototype.bind = function () {
    // unbind mousemove handler on mouseup
    $('body').on('mouseup.shamen', function (e) {
        $(window).off('mousemove.shamen');
    });
};
```

Now that have seen the $.mouseup handler binding, we need to fill in the details:

```
// bind mousedown event handler
Shamen.prototype.bind = function () {
    // filter on drag handle if developer defined one
    var selector = this.options.dragHandle || null;
    var self = this;
    // account for margins if element is position absolutely;
    // code reused from Duvet.js
    var parentMargins = this.$el.attr('position') === 'absolute' ?
        getMargins(this.$el.parent()[0]) : { top: 0, left: 0};

    // unbind mousemove handler on mouseup
    $('body').on('mouseup.shamen', function (e) {
        $(window).off('mousemove.shamen');
    });

    this.$el.on('mousedown.shamen', selector, function (e) {
        // get the initial mouse position
        var mousePos = {
            x: e.pageX,
            y: e.pageY
        };

        // bind mousemove event handler
        $(window).on('mousemove.shamen', function (e) {
            // get the differences between the mousedown position and the
            // positions from the mousemove events
            var xDiff = e.pageX - mousePos.x;
            var yDiff = e.pageY - mousePos.y;
            // get the draggable el's current position relative to the document
            var elPos = self.$el.offset();

            // apply the mouse position differences to the el's position
```

```
                self.$el.css({
                    top: elPos.top + yDiff,
                    left: elPos.left + xDiff,
                    position: 'absolute'
                });

                // store the current mouse position
                // to diff with the next mousemove positions
                mousePos = {
                    x: e.pageX,
                    y: e.pageY
                };
            });
        });
    };
```

Destroying a Draggable Instance

Like with the overlay widget and any other widget, it is always good practice to clean up. This helps to prevent memory leaks and reduces the possibility of a destroyed widget having an impact on the application (e.g., through a lingering node property or event handler):

```
// clean up to prevent memory leaks
Shamen.prototype.destroy = function () {
    // unbind mousedown
    this.$el.off('mousedown.shamen');
    // revert cursor for drag handle
    this.$dragHandle.css({ cursor: this.originalDragHandleCursor });

    // null out jQuery object, element references
    this.el = null;
    this.$el = null;
    this.$dragHandle = null;

    // revert options to defaults
    this.options = defaults;
};
```

Making the Dialog Widget Draggable

In some cases you may want a dialog to be draggable (for example, so that a user can see content that is obfuscated by the dialog). However, this may not always be the case, so making the dialog draggable will be optional.

We can use the following code to make our dialog widget draggable:

```
function Dialog (options) {
    // optionally clone dialog $el
    options.$el = options.clone ? $(options.$el).clone() :
        $(options.$el);
    // append to body
    if (options.appendToEl) {
        $(options.appendToEl).append(options.$el);
    }

    Voltron.call(this, options);

    // create a draggable instance
    if (options.draggable) {
        this.shamen = new Shamen(this.$el[0], {
            // dialog header is the drag handle
            dragHandle: '#title'
        });
    }

    // create overlay instance
    this.overlay = new Duvet(this.$el[0], {
        fixed: options.draggable ? false : true
    });

    return this;
}

Dialog.prototype.destroy = function () {
    // clean up overlay
    this.overlay.destroy();

    // clean up draggable
    if (this.shamen) {
        this.shamen.destroy();
    }

    // call superclass
    Voltron.prototype.destroy.call(this);
};
```

Summary

In this chapter we demystified how elements are moved along the x- and y-axes by a user via a mouse. This demystification involved understanding the relevant mouse events: mousedown, mousemove, and mouseup. We covered best practices for the different events, then used this knowledge to create a small library that could be used to make any element draggable. We then integrated this library into the dialog widget, so you know how to create a draggable dialog instance when a use case requires that the dialog be movable.

This was just one possible use case and implementation, but it highlighted common patterns that are useful in general when handling different mouse events. This knowledge is useful for other use cases too, such as creating drop-down menus, and we will leverage it in the next chapter to make elements resizable.

Resizing Elements

Jason Strimpel

Oftentimes in web applications you will see a drag handle, which is used to adjust the size of an element. This may be done to improve usability, or to support some functionality. For instance, the developer might make an element resizable to allow users to alter the line wrapping of text inside the element, to make it easier to read. A functional application could be for a matrix of elements that needs to be resized. In this chapter we will create a widget that can be used to make any element resizable. We will then integrate this widget into the dialog widget, so that dialog instances can optionally be made resizable.

Mouse Events and Best Practices (Recap)

The same mouse events and best practices described in Chapter 7 apply when resizing an element. If you are jumping around the book and did not read the previous chapter, you'll find a brief synopsis of the mouse events and best practices here (although I'd advise reading the previous chapter before going further!)

Events

jQuery supports eleven different mouse events (*http://bit.ly/dwc-jquery-mouse*). However, making an element draggable only requires understanding three of these events:

- `$.mousemove` is used to get the mouse coordinates. jQuery normalizes these in the event object as the properties `e.pageX` and `e.pageY`.

- `$.mousedown` is used to bind the `$.mousemove` handler and get the initial mouse coordinates.

- `$.mouseup` is used to unbind the `$mousemove` handler to prevent excessive `$mousemove` events from being triggered.

Best Practices

In addition to knowing the required mouse events for making an element resizable, it is equally important to know how to optimize the usage of these events. Here are a few best practices:

- Bind `$.mousemove` on `$.mousedown` to prevent unnecessary `mousemove` events from being triggered.
- Unbind `$.mousemove` on `$.mouseup` to prevent unnecessary `mousemove` events from being triggered.
- Bind the `$.mouseup` event handler to the `<body>`. The API documentation (*http://api.jquery.com/mousemove/*) recommends this because in some cases, "the `mouseup` event might be sent to a different HTML element than the `mousemove` event was."

Resizing an Element

The same basic mouse movement and positioning best practices that apply to dragging an element also apply to resizing an element. However, additional properties can be set depending on the direction of the resizing. There are eight different possible directions when resizing an element:

- North or top middle
- Northeast or top right
- East or middle right
- Southeast or bottom right
- South or bottom middle
- Southwest or bottom left
- West or middle left
- Northwest or top left

In the case of right (east) or bottom (south) resizing the element's `width` or `height` property is adjusted, respectively. In the case of left (west) or top (north) resizing the element's `left` or `top` property is adjusted, in addition to the `width` or `height` property.

The examples from this point forward will use position-based descriptors (top, left, bottom, and right) instead of direction-based descriptors (north, east, south, and west) as position-based descriptors relate directly to CSS positioning, which makes things easier for me to visualize. Also, I'm an engineer, not a navigator! The direction-based descriptors were listed because some libraries, such as jQuery UI (*https://jqueryui.com/*), use them. This is probably because they correspond with the cursor properties (*http://bit.ly/dwc-cursor*).

Making a Resizable API

As in the previous chapters, the first step is to stub out an API:

```
// Eh-neeek-chock
var ApacheChief = (function (global, $) {

    'use strict';

    // default resize handle CSS
    var handlesCss = {
        width: '10px',
        height: '10px',
        cursor: 'se-resize'
    };

    // options defaults
    var defaults = {
        handles: ['BR'],
        handlesCss: {
            BR: handlesCss
        }
    };

    // merge default CSS and developer-defined CSS -
    // this is necessary because $.extend is shallow
    function mergeResizeHandleCss(defaultCss, instanceCss) {

    }

    // create resizable instance
    function ApacheChief(el, options) {
        this.el = el;
        this.$el = $(el);
        // extend options with developer-defined options
        this.options = $.extend({}, defaults, options);

        // extend isn't deep, so ensure that resize handle CSS
        // is merged properly
        mergeResizeHandleCss(this.options, options || {});
```

```
        // create resize handles
        this.createResizeHandles();

        // bind event handlers
        this.bind();
    }

    // create resize handles
    ApacheChief.prototype.createResizeHandles = function () {

    };

    // resize function
    ApacheChief.prototype.resize = function () {

    };

    // bind event handlers
    ApacheChief.prototype.bind = function () {

    };

    // clean up instance
    ApacheChief.prototype.destroy = function () {

    };

    return ApacheChief;

})(window, jQuery);
```

Defining Drag Handles

In order for an element to be resizable, it must have drag handles. We can implement these via a function that accepts an element and positions object as arguments.

The first step is to merge any developer-defined resize handle CSS with the default CSS by filling in the mergeResizeHandleCss function defined in the API stub:

```
// merge default CSS and developer-defined CSS -
// this is necessary because $.extend is shallow
function mergeResizeHandleCss(defaultCss, instanceCss) {
    var retVal = {};

    // iterate over default CSS properties
    for (var k in defaultCss) {
        // set return value property equal to the instance property defined
        // by the developer or the default CSS property value; it is also
        // possible to go down one more layer, but this assumes wholesale
        // property replacement
```

```
            retVal[k] = instanceCss[k] || defaultCss[k];
    }

    return retVal;
}
```

The next step is to create the resize handles by creating new DOM elements and applying the resize handle CSS to these newly defined elements. These elements are then inserted into the DOM:

```
// create resize handles
ApacheChief.prototype.createResizeHandles = function () {
    var handlesCss = this.options.handlesCss;
    var handles = this.options.handles;
    var $handles;

    // loop the resize handles CSS hash, create elements,
    // and append them to this.$el
    // data-handle attribute is used to help determine what element
    // properties should be adjusted when resizing
    for (var i = 0; i < handles.length; i++) {
        if (handlesCss[handles[i]]) {
            this.$el
                .append($('<div class="apache-chief-resize" data-handle="' +
                handles[i] + '">')
                .css(handlesCss[handles[i]]));
        }
    }

    $handles = this.$el.find('.apache-chief-resize');
    // ensure that container is an offset parent for positioning handles
    if (this.$el !== $handles.offsetParent()) {
        this.$el.css('position', 'relative');
    }
    $handles.css('display', 'block');
};
```

Binding Event Handlers

The event handlers bound in `ApacheChief.prototype.bind` are very similar to the ones bound in `Shamen.prototype.bind` from the previous chapter and follow the same mouse events best practices.

$.mousedown Handler

In addition to capturing the initial mouse coordinates like the draggable `$.mousedown` handler, the resizable `$.mousedown` handler extracts the direction from the handle element, which was set by `ApacheChief.prototype.createResizeHandles`:

```
$('.apache-chief-resize').on('mousedown.apache-chief', function (e) {
    var $handle = $(this);
    var direction = $handle.attr('data-handle');
    // if true then the handle moves in a position
    // that only affects width and height
    var adjustPosition = direction !== 'BM' &&
        direction !== 'MR' && direction !== 'BR';
    // get the initial mouse position
    var mousePos = {
        x: e.pageX,
        y: e.pageY
    };

    // this will be used by the mousemove handler
    // get coordinates for resizing
    function getPositionDiffs(adjustPosition, e, mousePos, direction) {
        var diffs = {
            xDim: direction === 'BM' ? 0 : e.pageX - mousePos.x,
            yDim: direction === 'MR' ? 0 : e.pageY - mousePos.y,
            xPos: 0,
            yPos: 0
        };

        if (!adjustPosition) {
            return diffs;
        }

        switch (direction) {
            case 'TR':
                diffs.yPos = diffs.yDim;
                diffs.yDim = -diffs.yDim;
                break;
            case 'TL':
                diffs.xPos = diffs.xDim;
                diffs.xDim = -diffs.xDim;
                diffs.yPos = diffs.yDim;
                diffs.yDim = -diffs.yDim;
                break;
            case 'BL':
                diffs.xPos = diffs.xDim;
                diffs.xDim = -diffs.xDim;
                break;
            case 'ML':
                diffs.xPos = diffs.xDim;
                diffs.xDim = -diffs.xDim;
                diffs.yDim = 0;
                break;
            case 'TM':
                diffs.yPos = diffs.yDim;
                diffs.yDim = -diffs.yDim;
                diffs.xDim = 0;
                break;
```

```
        }
        return diffs;
    }
});
```

$.mousemove Handler

The $.mousemove handler is bound in the $.mousedown handler. Just like with the draggable $.mousemove handler, the previous mouse coordinates are subtracted from the current mouse coordinates. These values are then used to adjust the width and height properties and, depending on the resize direction, the top and left properties:

```
$(window).on('mousemove.apache-chief', function (e) {
    // get the differences between the mousedown position and the
    // positions from the mousemove events
    var diffs = getPositionDiffs(adjustPosition, e, mousePos, direction);
    // get the draggable el's current position relative to the document
    var elPos;

    // adjust the width and height
    self.$el.css({
        width: self.$el.width() + diffs.xDim,
        height: self.$el.height() + diffs.yDim
    });

    // adjust the top and left
    if (adjustPosition) {
        elPos = self.$el.offset();
        self.$el.css({
            top: elPos.top + diffs.yPos,
            left: elPos.left + diffs.xPos,
            position: 'absolute'
        });
    }

    // store the current mouse position
    // to diff with the next mousemove positions
    mousePos = {
        x: e.pageX,
        y: e.pageY
    };
});
```

$.mouseup Handler

The $.mouseup handler is bound to the <body>, per the best practices described in the previous chapter. It unbinds the $.mousemove handler to prevent unnecessary memory consumption (it is then rebound when the next mousedown event is captured on a resize handle):

```
$('body').on('mouseup.apache-chief', function (e) {
    $(window).off('mousemove.apache-chief');
});
```

Destroying a Resizable Instance

Just as with any other widget, it is good practice to clean up to help prevent memory leaks. In addition to nulling out the element references and unbinding the event handlers, we'll remove the drag handle elements from the DOM:

```
// clean up instance
ApacheChief.prototype.destroy = function () {
    this.$el.off('mousedown.apache-chief');
    // remove the resize handles
    this.$el.find('.apache-chief-resize').remove();

    this.el = null;
    this.$el = null;
    this.options = defaults;
};
```

Completed Resizing Library

A few parts were missing from the original API stub, such as the full definitions for the drag handles. These missing pieces, along with all the code from the previous sections, have been added here so that the widget can be easily viewed in its entirety:

```
// Eh-neeek-chock
var ApacheChief = (function (global, $) {

    'use strict';

    // default resize handle CSS
    var handlesCss = {
        width: '10px',
        height: '10px',
        cursor: 'se-resize',
        position: 'absolute',
        display: 'none',
        'background-color': '#000'
    };

    // options defaults
    var defaults = {
        handles: ['BR'],
        handlesCss: {
            TM: $.extend({}, handlesCss, {
                cursor: 'n-resize', top: 0, left: '50%'
            }),
```

```
        TR: $.extend({}, handlesCss, {
            cursor: 'ne-resize', top: 0, right: 0
        }),
        MR: $.extend({}, handlesCss, {
            cursor: 'e-resize', bottom: '50%', right: 0
        }),
        BR: $.extend({}, handlesCss, { bottom: 0, right: 0 }),
        BM: $.extend({}, handlesCss, {
            cursor: 's-resize', bottom: 0, left: '50%'
        }),
        ML: $.extend({}, handlesCss, {
            cursor: 'w-resize', bottom: '50%', left: 0
        }),
        BL: $.extend({}, handlesCss, {
            cursor: 'sw-resize', bottom: 0, left: 0
        }),
        TL: $.extend({}, handlesCss, { cursor: 'nw-resize' }),
    }
};

// merge default CSS and developer-defined CSS -
// this is necessary because $.extend is shallow
function mergeResizeHandleCss(defaultCss, instanceCss) {
    var retVal = {};

    // iterate over default CSS properties
    for (var k in defaultCss) {
        // set return value property equal to the instance property defined
        // by the developer or the default CSS property value; it is also
        // possible to go down one more layer, but this assumes wholesale
        // property replacement
        retVal[k] = instanceCss[k] || defaultCss[k];
    }

    return retVal;
}

// create resizable instance
function ApacheChief(el, options) {
    this.el = el;
    this.$el = $(el);
    // extend options with developer-defined options
    this.options = $.extend({}, defaults, options);

    // extend isn't deep, so ensure that resize handle CSS is merged
    // properly
    mergeResizeHandleCss(this.options, options || {});

    // create resize handles
    this.createResizeHandles();

    // bind event handlers
```

```
            this.bind();
    }

    // create resize handles
    ApacheChief.prototype.createResizeHandles = function () {
        var handlesCss = this.options.handlesCss;
        var handles = this.options.handles;
        var $handles;

        // loop the resize handles CSS hash, create elements,
        // and append them to this.$el
        // data-handle attribute is used to help determine what element
        // properties should be adjusted when resizing
        for (var i = 0; i < handles.length; i++) {
            if (handlesCss[handles[i]]) {
                this.$el
                    .append($('<div class="apache-chief-resize" data-handle="' +
                    handles[i] + '">')
                    .css(handlesCss[handles[i]]));
            }
        }

        $handles = this.$el.find('.apache-chief-resize');
        // ensure that container is an offset parent for positioning handles
        if (this.$el !== $handles.offsetParent()) {
            this.$el.css('position', 'relative');
        }
        $handles.css('display', 'block');
    };

    // bind event handlers
    ApacheChief.prototype.bind = function () {
        var self = this;

        $('body').on('mouseup.apache-chief', function (e) {
            $(window).off('mousemove.apache-chief');
        });

        this.$el.find('.apache-chief-resize').on('mousedown.apache-chief',
            function (e) {
            var $handle = $(this);
            var direction = $handle.attr('data-handle');
            // if true then the handle moves in a position
            // that only affects width and height
            var adjustPosition = direction !== 'BM' &&
                direction !== 'MR' && direction !== 'BR';
            // get the initial mouse position
             var mousePos = {
                x: e.pageX,
                y: e.pageY
            };
```

```
// get coordinates for resizing
function getPositionDiffs(adjustPosition, e, mousePos, direction) {
    var diffs = {
        xDim: direction === 'BM' ? 0 : e.pageX - mousePos.x,
        yDim: direction === 'MR' ? 0 : e.pageY - mousePos.y,
        xPos: 0,
        yPos: 0
    };

    if (!adjustPosition) {
        return diffs;
    }

    switch (direction) {
        case 'TR':
            diffs.yPos = diffs.yDim;
            diffs.yDim = -diffs.yDim;
            break;
        case 'TL':
            diffs.xPos = diffs.xDim;
            diffs.xDim = -diffs.xDim;
            diffs.yPos = diffs.yDim;
            diffs.yDim = -diffs.yDim;
            break;
        case 'BL':
            diffs.xPos = diffs.xDim;
            diffs.xDim = -diffs.xDim;
            break;
        case 'ML':
            diffs.xPos = diffs.xDim;
            diffs.xDim = -diffs.xDim;
            diffs.yDim = 0;
            break;
        case 'TM':
            diffs.yPos = diffs.yDim;
            diffs.yDim = -diffs.yDim;
            diffs.xDim = 0;
            break;
    }

    return diffs;
}

$(window).on('mousemove.apache-chief', function (e) {
    // get the differences between the mousedown position and the
    // positions from the mousemove events
    var diffs = getPositionDiffs(adjustPosition, e, mousePos,
        direction);
    // get the draggable el's current position relative to the
    // document
    var elPos;
```

```
            // adjust the width and height
            self.$el.css({
                width: self.$el.width() + diffs.xDim,
                height: self.$el.height() + diffs.yDim
            });

            // adjust the top and left
            if (adjustPosition) {
                elPos = self.$el.offset();
                self.$el.css({
                    top: elPos.top + diffs.yPos,
                    left: elPos.left + diffs.xPos,
                    position: 'absolute'
                });
            }

            // store the current mouse position
            // to diff with the next mousemove positions
            mousePos = {
                x: e.pageX,
                y: e.pageY
            };
        });
    });
};

// clean up instance
ApacheChief.prototype.destroy = function () {
    this.$el.off('mousedown.apache-chief');
    // remove the resize handles
    this.$el.find('.apache-chief-resize').remove();

    this.el = null;
    this.$el = null;
    this.options = defaults;
};

return ApacheChief;

})(window, jQuery);
```

Making the Dialog Widget Resizable

In some cases you may want a dialog widget instance to be resizable, so that a user
can better interact with the dialog's content. For instance, it could be that a form that
would normally fit within the dialog could have fields dynamically appended to it
depending on a user's actions, causing it to overflow. Making the dialog resizable
would make it much easier for the user to view and interact with all the form fields
without having to scroll.

We can use the following code to make our dialog widget resizable:

```javascript
function Dialog (options) {
    // optionally clone dialog $el
    options.$el = options.clone ? $(options.$el).clone() :
        $(options.$el);
    // append to body
    if (options.appendToEl) {
        $(options.appendToEl).append(options.$el);
    }

    Voltron.call(this, options);

    // create a draggable instance
    if (options.draggable) {
        this.shamen = new Shamen(this.$el[0], {
            // dialog header is the drag handle
            dragHandle: '#title'
        });
    }

    // create a resizable instance
    if (options.resizable) {
        this.apacheChief = new ApacheChief(this.$el[0], {
            handles: ['BR']
        });
    }

    // create overlay instance
    this.overlay = new Duvet(this.$el[0], {
        fixed: options.draggable ? false : true
    });

    return this;
}

Dialog.prototype.destroy = function () {
    // clean up overlay
    this.overlay.destroy();

    // clean up draggable
    if (this.shamen) {
        this.shamen.destroy();
    }

    // clean up resizable
    if (this.apacheChief) {
        this.apacheChief.destroy();
    }

    // call superclass
    Voltron.prototype.destroy.call(this);
};
```

Summary

In this chapter we examined the events and patterns used to implement a drag handle on an element to make it resizable. We encapsulated this knowledge into a reusable widget that we then incorporated into the dialog widget, making it optionally resizable.

The information in this chapter enhanced the knowledge gained from the previous chapter, providing a richer understanding of handling mouse events. For more information on the mouse events from these chapters and others, please refer to the MDN documentation (*http://bit.ly/dwc-mdn*) and the jQuery documentation (*http://bit.ly/dwc-jquery-mouse*) on mouse events.

Completing the Dialog Widget

Jason Strimpel

This chapter focuses on completing the dialog widget that will be used throughout the rest of the book.

Styling the Widget

I am not a UI/UX expert, nor am I a designer. The selected styles were based on the default styling for jQuery UI. The drag handle image is a portion of a jQuery UI sprite as well.

The intent of this styling is not to advise on styling in the sense of aesthetics or usability, but rather to describe how to apply any styles to a widget.

Adding CSS

The dialog CSS is very minimal. It could easily be stored internally in the dialog widget JavaScript and then applied directly to the elements in question upon instantiation of a dialog widget. However, this approach would not scale well or lend itself to ease of maintenance.

For instance, if you wanted to add a positioned background image it would require setting each property individually as opposed to being able to simply apply all styling in the value of the background property of a selector in a stylesheet. Additionally, applying the CSS via JavaScript is not nearly as efficient as allowing the browser to apply the styles defined in a stylesheet. Lastly, it makes overriding the CSS properties more difficult—because the CSS is applied inline if done via JavaScript, a higher level of specificity is required than when overriding CSS set in a stylesheet.

With those caveats in mind, here's the CSS for our simple dialog widget:

```css
[role="dialog"] {
    display: none;
}

[role="dialog"] {
    width: 400px;
    height: 200px;
    position: absolute;
    border: 1px solid #bbb;
    border-radius: 5px;
    font-family: "Trebuchet MS", "Helvetica", "Arial", "Verdana", "sans-serif";
}

[role="dialog"] h2 {
    background: #bbb;
    font-size: 16px;
    font-weight: normal;
    padding: 10px;
    margin: 3px;
    border-radius: 5px;
    padding: 5px;
    color: #eee;
}

[role="dialog"] p {
    margin: 0;
    padding: 10px;
    font-size: 12px;
    color: #333;
}
```

I reserve using `!important` for state overrides such as error messages, to ensure that the proper error styling takes effect regardless of specificity, and overriding the styles set via JavaScript (inline styles). In this case we are overriding one of the latter, which is being set by `ApacheChief`:

```css
[role="dialog"] .apache-chief-resize {
    background: url(jquery-ui-icons.png) -64px -224px !important;
    width: 16px !important;
    height: 16px !important;
}
```

Concatenating the JavaScript

The JavaScript was concatenated using `grunt-preprocess` (*https://github.com/jsover son/grunt-preprocess*). The dialog widget dependencies were included inside a closure so as to create the minimal global footprint:

```
(function (global, $) {

    // @include components/jquery/dist/jquery.sj
    // @include components/chapter-6_duvet/duvet.js
    // @include components/chapter-7_shamen/shamen.js
    // @include components/chapter-8_apache-chief/apacheChief.js
    // @include components/chapter-2_voltron/voltron.js
    // @include dialog.js

})(window, jQuery);
```

Summary

Congratulations—you now have a fully functioning dialog widget! More importantly, you have a better understanding of how other UI libraries implement similar components. This understanding was gained by breaking the dialog widget into smaller, reusable widgets, each of which handled a specific requirement (resizing, dragging, cloning, etc.). Armed with this knowledge you now have an understanding of "one layer of abstraction below your everyday work," so you can make more informed design and implementation decisions. The end result is the development of better software and easier maintenance of this software, which will make you a more productive and happier engineer. And doesn't everyone want to be happier?

Building HTML5 Web Components

Part I of this book provided an understanding of how a browser lays out a page by introducing normal flow, positioning, and stacking contexts. Part II described how to use this understanding to manipulate the properties that affect the aforementioned topics to control a page's layout. This knowledge was then used to create small widgets with specific purposes that could be combined to create a larger UI widget, the dialog example. However, these widgets are not web components as described by the W3C (*http://www.w3.org/TR/components-intro/*). They were designed to function within the current context of the Web. Part III is all about true web components and the benefits they offer. It will cover the parts that comprise the W3C Web Components specification, templates, custom elements, the shadow DOM, and imports. As part of this learning process, in this section of the book we will take the dialog widget from Parts I and II and convert it to a bona fide web component, making it more semantic, declarative, encapsulated, consumable, and maintainable. More importantly, here we will truly extend the web platform for the first time.

Utilizing Templates

Jason Strimpel

As you read the title of this chapter you might have thought to yourself, "But we already have client-side templates for rendering markup!" Here's an example:

```
<script id="some-template" type="text/x-handlebars-template">
    <p class="description">{{description}}</p>
</script>

<div id="some-template" style="display: none;">
    <p class="description">{{description}}</p>
</div>

function (Handlebars,depth0,helpers,partials,data) {
  this.compilerInfo = [4,'>= 1.0.0'];
helpers = this.merge(helpers, Handlebars.helpers); data = data || {};
  var buffer = "", stack1, helper, functionType="function",
  escapeExpression=this.escapeExpression;


  buffer += "<div id=\"some-template\" style=\"display: none;\">";
  buffer += "<p class=\"description\">";
  if (helper = helpers.description) {
  stack1 = helper.call(depth0, {hash:{},data:data}); }
  else { helper = (depth0 && depth0.description);
  stack1 = typeof helper === functionType ?
  helper.call(depth0, {hash:{},data:data}) : helper; }
  buffer += escapeExpression(stack1)
    + "</p></div>";
  return buffer;
  }
```

While these approaches allow you to utilize templates on the client, they have their drawbacks. This is because they are really just workarounds designed to implement a missing feature: native templates in the browser. The good news is that this feature is no longer missing. It is now a W3C specification (*http://bit.ly/dwc-w3c-html*) and is running in some of the latest browser versions. This new specification will allow you to begin writing native templates in a standardized fashion that are specifically designed to work more efficiently with the browser.

 Eric Bidelman has created a significant amount of the web component content on the Web outside of the W3C specifications. Eric's postings and the W3C specifications were the primary sources for the majority of Part III, including this chapter. A big thanks to Eric and the many others who have been posting and speaking on this topic for helping to drive our learning.

Understanding the Importance of Templates

Many different template solutions currently exist in the market: Handlebars (*http://handlebarsjs.com/*), Dust (*https://github.com/linkedin/dustjs*), Nunjucks (*http://mozilla.github.io/nunjucks/*), micro templating (*http://underscorejs.org/#template*), etc. While these are useful and amazing solutions, they are only templates in a limited sense. They provide functionality similar to their server-side counterparts, compiling strings to functions. These functions then take data and output strings comprised of the original strings with the data substituted per the template tokens and processing rules. This functionality is extremely important, but the browser is a much different environment than the server. Since it is a different environment, it requires different features and optimizations.

 Native templates are not a replacement for existing template solutions. They are just a standardized way to get a chunk of markup to the browser and have it remain inert until it is needed. Per the W3C Web Components specification (*http://bit.ly/dwc-w3c-webcomp*), "The `<template>` element has a property called `content` which holds the content of the template in a document fragment. When the author wants to use the content they can move or copy the nodes from this property."

Deferring the Processing of Resources

One of the optimizations that templates afford is the deferment of the processing of assets such as scripts and images. This delay of processing allows developers to include as many templates as they want with virtually no impact on the rendering of the page (although transferring larger files over the network will, of course, affect the time to render).

Deferring the Rendering of Content

In addition to deferring the processing of assets, template markup is not rendered by the browser, regardless of where the template is located. This allows a developer to place templates in any location and conditionally render them without the need to toggle display properties or be concerned about the overhead of parsing markup not used by the browser.

Hiding the Content from the DOM

The template content is also not considered to be part of the DOM. When a query is made for DOM nodes, none of the template child nodes are returned. This ensures that templates do not slow down node lookups and that template content remains hidden until it is activated.

Creating and Using a Template

A template is created by adding a <template> to the markup, selecting the template node, cloning its content, and then inserting the cloned content into the DOM.

Detecting Browser Support

In order to make use of native templates, the first step is to determine if a browser supports them. This check can then be used to implement a polyfill to support templates in older browsers:

```
var supportsTemplates = (function () {
    return 'content' in document.createElement('template');
})();
```

Placing a Template in Markup

A template is created by adding a <template> tag to a <head>, <body>, or <frameset>, or any descendant tag of the aforementioned tags:

```
<head>
    <template id="atcq">
        <p class="response"></p>
        <script type="text/javascript">
            (function () {
                var p = confirm('You on point Tip?');
                var responeEl = document.querySelector('.response');

                if (p) {
                    responeEl.innerHTML = 'All the time Phife';
                } else {
                    responeEl.innerHTML = 'Check the rhyme y\'all';
                }
```

```
                })();
            </script>
        </template>
    </head>
```

Adding a Template to the DOM

To add a template to the DOM and render it, you must first get a reference to the template node. Then you need to make a copy of the node, and finally add the new node to the DOM:

```
// get a reference to the template node
var template = document.querySelector('#atcq');
// clone it
var templateClone = document.importNode(template.content, true);
// append the cloned content to the DOM
document.body.appendChild(templateClone);
```

Converting the Dialog Component to a Template

Converting the dialog component to a template is done by taking the JavaScript, CSS, and HTML required to render the dialog, and embedding it inside a `<template>` tag. This will make the JavaScript and CSS inert until the template is cloned and added to the DOM. Our dialog template looks like this:

```
<head>
    <script type="text/javascript" src="/vendor/jquery.js"></script>
    <template id="dialog">
        <style>
            // styling src
        </style>
        <script type="text/javascript">
            // dialog component source
        </script>
        <div role="dialog" aria-labelledby="title" aria-describedby="content">
            <h2 id="title">I am a title</h2>
            <p id="content">Look at me! I am content.</p>
        </div>
    </template>
</head>
```

This template injects the inert resources into the DOM, but it does not provide a convenient API for developers to leverage the dialog component. If the template and the dialog component it contains is to be reused, then an API for accessing the dialog component must be created.

You may have noticed that the template is embedding scripts directly as opposed to using the `src` attribute to import them. That is because any `script` added to the DOM after the document has been parsed loads sources asynchronously. Per the W3C HTML5 specification (*http://bit.ly/dwc-w3c-script*), one of the pieces of state associated with a `script` element is "a flag indicating whether the element will 'force-async'. Initially, `script` elements must have this flag set. It is unset by the HTML parser and the XML parser on `script` elements they insert." If the scripts were not embedded a number of possible errors could occur, as the resources would not be available until the scripts had completed loading.

Creating a Wrapper API for the Dialog Template

If you want to encapsulate cloning and appending the template, then it is best to create a wrapper constructor function that encapsulates this logic along with the dialog component instantiation. This encapsulation also allows you to embed optimizations such as only cloning the template once:

```
function DialogTemplate(options) {
    this.querySelector = '[role="dialog"]';
    this.template = document.querySelector('#dialog');
    this.el = document.querySelector(this.querySelector);
    this.options = options;

    // only import and append once
    if (!this.el) {
        this.clone = document.importNode(this.template.content, true);
        document.body.appendChild(this.clone);
        this.el = document.querySelector('[role="dialog"]');
    }

    // create dialog instance
    this.options.$el = this.querySelector;
    this.api = new Dialog(this.options);

    // set the title and content for the dialog
    this.api.$el.find('#title').html(this.options.title);
    this.api.$el.find('#content').html(this.options.content);

    return this;
}
```

Instantiating a Dialog Component Instance

The dialog component can now be instantiated as before, but now it will be done from the template using the new wrapper constructor function:

```
var dialog = new DialogTemplate({
    draggable: true,
    resizable: true,
});
dialog.api.show();
```

Abstracting the Dialog Template Wrapper

The dialog component wrapper constructor function was specific to the dialog component. If you would like to create a more generic wrapper, it is possible. The trade-offs are that all your templates have to expose the same public API with the same signature, and you cannot encapsulate optimization logic inside of the wrapper constructor function. A generic template wrapper might look like the following:

```
// assumes that all templates return a public
// API that has the same signature
var templateFactory = (function (window) {

    'use strict';

    return function (template, API) {
        function Template(options, callback) {
            var self = this;

            this.options = options;
            // clone template content
            this.clone = document.importNode(this.template.content, true);
            // append cloned template content to target el
            options.target.appendChild(this.clone);
            // get el for public API exposed by appending template
            this.el = document.querySelector(options.$root);
            options.$el = this.el;

            // assumes that template adds public API
            // to the window and that API uses a
            // constructor to create new instance
            self.api = new window[self.API](options);

            return this;
        }

        TemplateAPI.prototype.template = template;
        TemplateAPI.prototype.API = API;
```

```
        return Template;
    };

})(window);
```

Summary

In this chapter we covered web component templates as defined by the W3C. First, we discussed the benefits these templates afford over the current template solutions (similar to their server-side counterparts):

- The processing of resources such as images and tags is deferred, so they do not impact performance in that respect (any additional content sent across the network always decreases performance).
- The rendering of content is deferred; content is not rendered unless it is explicitly added to the DOM.
- Template content is hidden from the DOM, so it does not slow down query selections.

Then we created a template and imported it into the DOM. Next, we took the dialog component and made it into a template. Finally, we created a wrapper for instantiating dialog components from the dialog component template node and examined converting the dialog component template into a factory function that could be used to wrap any template that returned an API that subscribed to the contract defined in the template wrapper code.

Working with the Shadow DOM

Jason Strimpel

The shadow DOM is not the dark side of the DOM, but if it were I would definitely give in to my hatred of the lack of encapsulation the DOM normally affords and cross over.

One of the aspects of the DOM that makes development of widgets/components difficult is this lack of encapsulation. For instance, one major problem has always been CSS rules bleeding into or out of a component's branch of the DOM tree: it forces one to write overly specific selectors or abuse `!important` so that styles do not conflict, and even then conflicts still happen in large applications. Another issue caused by lack of encapsulation is that code external to a component can still traverse into the component's branch of the DOM tree. These problems and others can be prevented by using the shadow DOM.

What Is the Shadow DOM?

So what exactly is this mysterious-sounding shadow DOM? According to the W3C (*http://www.w3.org/TR/components-intro/*):

> Shadow DOM is an adjunct tree of DOM nodes. These shadow DOM subtrees can be associated with an element, but do not appear as child nodes of the element. Instead the subtrees form their own scope. For example, a shadow DOM subtree can contain IDs and styles that overlap with IDs and styles in the document, but because the shadow DOM subtree (unlike the child node list) is separate from the document, the IDs and styles in the shadow DOM subtree do not clash with those in the document.

I am an admirer of the W3C, but oftentimes their specifications, albeit accurate, need to be translated into something that the rest of us—myself included—can more easily comprehend. The shadow DOM is essentially a way to define a new DOM tree whose root container, or host, is visible in the document, while the shadow root and its children are not. Think of it as a way to create isolated DOM trees to prevent collisions such as duplicate identifiers, or accidental modifications by broad query selectors. That is a simplification, but it should help to illustrate the purpose.

So what benefits does the shadow DOM provide to developers? It essentially provides encapsulation for a subtree from the parent page. This subtree can contain markup, CSS, JavaScript, or any asset that can be included in a web page. This allows you to create widgets without being concerned that of any of the assets will impact the parent page, or vice versa. Previously this level of encapsulation was only achievable by using an <iframe>.

Shadow DOM Basics

The shadow DOM is a simple concept, but it has some intricacies that make it appear more complex than it really is. This section will focus on the basics. The intricacies that afford the developer even more control and power will be covered later in this chapter.

Shadow Host

A shadow host is a DOM node that contains a shadow root. It is a regular element node within the parent page that hosts the scoped shadow subtree. Any child nodes that reside under the shadow host are still selectable, with the exception of the shadow root.

Shadow Root

A shadow root is an element that gets added to a shadow host. The shadow root is the root node for the shadow DOM branch. Shadow root child nodes are not returned by DOM queries even if a child node matches the given query selector. Creating a shadow root on a node in the parent page makes the node upon which it was created a shadow host.

Creating a shadow root

Creating a shadow root is a straightforward process. First a shadow host node is selected, and then a shadow root is created in the shadow host.

To inspect shadow DOM branches using the Chrome debugger, check the "Show Shadow DOM" box under the "Elements" section in the "General" settings panel of the debugger.

The code to create a shadow root looks like this:

```
<div id="host"></div>

var host = document.querySelector('#host');
var root = host.createShadowRoot();
```

If you do not prefix createShadowRoot with "webkit" in Chrome 34 and below you are going to have a bad time (*http://caniuse.com/ shadowdom*). All calls to createShadowRoot should look like host.webkitCreateShadowRoot().

It is possible to attach multiple shadow roots to a single shadow host. However, only the last shadow root attached is rendered. A shadow host follows the LIFO pattern (last in, first out) when attaching shadow roots. At this point you might be asking yourself, "So what is the point of hosting multiple shadow roots if only the last one attached is rendered?" Excellent question, but you are getting ahead of the game! This will be covered later in this chapter (see "Shadow Insertion Points" on page 120).

Using a Template with the Shadow DOM

Using a template to populate a shadow root involves almost the same process as using a template to add content to a DOM node in the parent page. The only difference is that the template.content is added to the shadow root.

The first step is to create a template node. This example leverages the template from the previous chapter, with the addition of an element that will be the shadow host:

```
<head>
    <template id="atcq">
        <p class="response"></p>
        <script type="text/javascript">
            (function () {
                var p = confirm('You on point Tip?');
                var responeEl = document.querySelector('#atcq-root')
                    .shadowRoot
                    .querySelector('.response');

                if (p) {
                    responeEl.innerHTML = 'All the time Phife';
                } else {
                    responeEl.innerHTML = 'Check the rhyme y\'all';
```

```
            }
        })();
    </script>
    </template>
</head>
<body>
    <div id="atcq-root"></div>
</body>
```

Next, we create a shadow root using the shadow host element, get a reference to the template node, and finally append the template content to the shadow root:

```
// create a shadow root
var root = document.querySelector('#atcq-root').createShadowRoot();
// get a reference to the template node
var template = document.querySelector('#atcq');
// append the cloned content to the shadow root
root.appendChild(template.content);
```

Shadow DOM Styling

I cannot count the number of times I have encountered CSS scoping issues throughout my career. Some of them were due to broad selectors such as div, the overusage of !important, or improperly namespaced CSS. Other times it has been difficult to override widget CSS or widget CSS has bled out, impacting application-level CSS. As an application grows in size, especially if multiple developers are working on the code base, it becomes even more difficult to prevent these problems. Good standards can help to mitigate these issues, but most applications leverage open source libraries such as jQuery UI, Kendo UI, Bootstrap, and others, which makes good standards alone inadequate. Addressing these problems and providing a standard way of applying styles to scoped elements are two of the benefits of using a shadow DOM.

Style Encapsulation

Any styles defined in the shadow DOM are scoped to the shadow root. They are not applied to any elements outside of this scope, even if their selector matches an element in the parent page. Styles defined outside of a shadow DOM are not applied to elements in the shadow root either.

In the example that follows, the text within the <p> that resides outside of the shadow root will be blue because that style is external to the shadow DOM that is created. The text within the <p> that is a child node of the shadow root will initially be the default color. This is because the styles defined outside of the shadow root are not applied to elements within the shadow root. After two seconds, the text within the <p> inside the shadow root will turn green, because the callback for the setTimeout function injects a <style> tag into the shadow root. The text within the <p> that resides outside of the shadow root will remain blue because the style injected into the shadow root is scoped to elements that are children of the shadow root. Here's the code that achieves this styling:

```
<head>
    <style>
        p {
            color: blue;
        }
    </style>
    <template><p>I am the default color, then green.</p></template>
</head>
<body>
    <div id="host"></div>
    <p>I am blue.</p>
    <script type="text/javascript">
        var template = document.querySelector('template');
        var root = document.querySelector('#host').createShadowRoot();

        root.appendChild(template.content);
        setTimeout(function () {
            root.innerHTML += '<style>p { color: green; }</style>';
        }, 2000)
    </script>
</body>
```

Styling the Host Element

In some cases you will want to style the host element itself. This is easily accomplished by creating a style anywhere within the parent page, because the host element is not part of the shadow root. This works fine, but what if you have a shadow host that needs different styling depending on the contents of the shadow root? And what if you have multiple shadow hosts that need to be styled based on their contents? As you can imagine, this would get very difficult to maintain. Fortunately, there is a new selector, :host, that provides access to the shadow host from within the shadow root. This allows you to encapsulate your host styling to the shadow root:

```
<head>
    <template id="template">
        <style>
            :host {
                border: 1px solid red;
                padding: 10px;
            }
        </style>
        My host element will have a red border!
    </template>
</head>
<body>
    <div id="host"></div>
    <script type="text/javascript">
        var template = document.querySelector('#template')
```

```
        var root = document.querySelector('#host').createShadowRoot();
        root.appendChild(template.content);
    </script>
</body>
```

The parent page selector has a higher specificity than the :host selector, so it will trump any shadow host styles defined within the shadow root:

```
<head>
    <style>
        #host {
            border: 1px solid green;
        }
    </style>
    <template id="template">
        <style>
            :host {
                border: 1px solid red;
                padding: 10px;
            }
        </style>
        My host element will have a green border!
    </template>
</head>
<body>
    <div id="host"></div>
    <script type="text/javascript">
        var template = document.querySelector('#template')
        var root = document.querySelector('#host').createShadowRoot();
        root.appendChild(template.content);
    </script>
</body>
```

If you want to override styles set in the parent page, this must be done inline on the host element:

```
<head>
    <template id="template">
        <style>
            :host {
                border: 1px solid red;
                padding: 10px;
            }
        </style>
        My host element will have a blue border!
    </template>
</head>
<body>
    <div id="host" style="border: 1px solid blue;"></div>
    <script type="text/javascript">
        var template = document.querySelector('#template')
        var root = document.querySelector('#host').createShadowRoot();
        root.appendChild(template.content);
```

```
    </script>
  </body>
```

The `:host` selector also has a functional form that accepts a selector, `:host selector`, allowing you to set styles for specific hosts. This functionality is useful for theming and managing states on the host element.

Styling Shadow Root Elements from the Parent Page

Encapsulation is all well and good, but what if you want to target specific shadow root elements with a styling update? What if you want to reuse templates and shadow host elements in a completely different application? What if you do not have control over the shadow root's content? For instance, you could be pulling the code from a repository that is maintained by another department internal to your organization, or a shared repository that is maintained by an external entity. In either case you might not have control over the shadow root's contents, or the update process might take a significant amount of time, which would block your development. Additionally, you might not *want* control over the content. Sometimes it is best to let domain experts maintain certain modules and to simply override the default module styling to suit your needs. Fortunately, the drafters of the W3C specification thought of these cases (and probably many more), so they created a selector that allows you to apply styling to shadow root elements from the parent page.

The `::shadow` pseudoelement selects the shadow root, allowing you to target child elements within the selected shadow root:

```
<head>
    <style>
        #host::shadow p {
            color: blue;
        }
    </style>
    <template><p>I am blue.</p></template>
</head>
<body>
    <div id="host"></div>
    <script type="text/javascript">
        var template = document.querySelector('template');
        var root = document.querySelector('#host').createShadowRoot();

        root.appendChild(template.content);
    </script>
</body>
```

The `::shadow` pseudoelement selector can be used to style nested shadow roots:

```
<head>
    <style>
        #parent-host::shadow #child-host::shadow p {
            color: blue;
```

```
        }
    </style>
    <template id="child-template"><p>I am blue.</p></template>
    <template id="parent-template">
        <p>I am the default color.</p>
        <div id="child-host"></div>
    </template>
</head>
<body>
    <div id="parent-host"></div>
    <script type="text/javascript">
        var parentTemplate = document.querySelector('#parent-template');
        var childTemplate = document.querySelector('#child-template');
        var parentRoot = document.querySelector('#parent-host')
            .createShadowRoot();
        var childRoot;

        parentRoot.appendChild(parentTemplate.content);
        childRoot = parentRoot.querySelector('#child-host').createShadowRoot();
        childRoot.appendChild(childTemplate.content);
    </script>
</body>
```

Sometimes targeting individual shadow roots using the ::shadow pseudoelement is very inefficient, especially if you are applying a theme to an entire application of shadow roots. Again, the drafters of the W3C specification had the foresight to anticipate this use case and specified the /deep/ combinator. The /deep/ combinator allows you cross through all shadow roots with a single selector:

```
<style>
    /* colors all <p> text within all shadow roots blue */
    body /deep/ p {
        color: blue;
    }

    /* colors all <p> text within the child shadow root blue */
    #parent-host /deep/ #child-host # p {
        color: blue;
    }

    /* targets a library theme/skin */
    body /deep/ p.skin {
        color: blue;
    }
</style>
```

At this point you might be asking yourself, "Doesn't this defeat the purpose of encapsulation?" But encapsulation does not mean putting up an impenetrable force field that makes crossing boundaries for appropriate use cases, such as theming UI components, impossible. The problem with the Web is that it has never had a formalized method of encapsulation or a defined API for breaking through an encapsulated component, like in other development platforms. The formalization of encapsulation and associated methods makes it clear in the code what the developer's intent is when encapsulation is breached. It also helps to prevent the bugs that plague a web platform that lacks formalized encapsulation.

Content Projection

One of the main tenets of web development best practices is the separation of content from presentation, the rationale being that it makes application maintenance easier and more accessible.

In the past separation of content from presentation has simply meant not placing styling details in markup. The shadow DOM takes this principle one step further.

In the examples we have seen thus far the content has been contained within a template and injected into the shadow root. In these examples no significant changes were made to the presentation, other than the text color. Most cases are not this simple.

In some cases it is necessary to place the content inside of the shadow host element for maintenance and accessibility purposes. However, that content needs to be projected into the shadow root in order to be presented. Luckily, the building blocks for projecting the content from the shadow host into the shadow root exist.

Projection via a Content Tag

One way to project content from the shadow host into the shadow root is by using a <content> element inside of a <template>. Any content inside the shadow host will be automatically projected into the <content> of the <template> used to compose the shadow root:

```
<head>
    <meta charset="utf-8">
    <title>Test Code</title>
    <template>
        <p>I am NOT projected content.</p>
        <content></content>
    </template>
</head>
<body>
```

```
<div id="host">
    <p>I am projected content.</p>
</div>
<script type="text/javascript">
    var template = document.querySelector('template');
    var root = document.querySelector('#host').createShadowRoot();

    root.appendChild(template.content);
</script>
</body>
```

Projection via Content Selectors

In some cases you may not want to project all of the content from the shadow host. You might want to select specific content for injection in different <content> elements in the shadow root. A common case is that some markup in the shadow host has semantic meaning and helps with accessibility, but doesn't add anything to the presentation of the shadow root. The mechanism for extracting content from the shadow host is the select attribute. This attribute can be added to a <content> element with a query selector value that will match an element in the shadow host. The matched element's content is then injected into the <content> tag.

 Only the first element matched by a <content> element's select attribute is injected into the element—keep this in mind when using selectors that are likely to match a number of elements, such as tag selectors (e.g., div).

The following example is a product listing with a review widget. The shadow host contains semantic markup that is accessible, and the template contains the presentation details. The template presentation does not lend itself well to accessibility and contains extraneous markup that is used for presentation purposes only—e.g., the column containers are there for positioning purposes only and the review <ul> items do not contain text (the interface would be purely graphical). In this example, select attributes are used in the <template> <content> elements to extract content from the shadow root:

```
<!--
    Only the relevant markup is shown. All other details,
    such as template CSS and JavaScript, have been omitted,
    so that the focus is on the selector projection use case.
-->
<template>
    <div class="product">
        <div class="column main">
            <content select="h2"></content>
            <content select=".description"></content>
        </div>
```

```
        <div class="column sidebar">
            <content select="h3"></content>
            <ul class="ratings">
                <li class="1-star"></li>
                <li class="2-star"></li>
                <li class="3-star"></li>
                <li class="4-star"></li>
            </ul>
        </div>
    </div>
</template>
<div id="host" class="product">
    <h2>ShamWow</h2>
    <p class="description">
        ShamWow washes, dries, and polishes any surface. It's like a towel,
        chamois, and sponge all in one!
    </p>
    <h3>Ratings</h3>
    <ul class="ratings">
        <li>1 star</li>
        <li>2 stars</li>
        <li>3 stars</li>
        <li>4 stars</li>
    </ul>
</div>
```

 Only nodes that are children of the shadow host can be projected, so you cannot select content from any lower descendant in the shadow host.

Getting Distributed Nodes and Insertion Points

Nodes that are projected from a host are referred to as *distributed nodes*. These nodes do not actually move locations in the DOM, which makes sense because the same host child node can be projected to different insertion points across shadow roots. As you can imagine, things can get complicated rather quickly, and at times you may need to do some inspecting and take action on distributed nodes in your application. There are two different methods that support this, Element.getDistributedNodes and Element.getDestinationInsertionPoints.

You cannot traverse into a <content> tree, because a <content> node does not have any descendant nodes. It is helpful to think of a <content> node as a television that is displaying a program. The television's only role in producing the program is to display it. The program itself was filmed and edited elsewhere for consumption by an unlimited number of televisions.

We use these methods as follows:

```
// Element.getDistributedNodes
var root = document.querySelector('#some-host').createShadowRoot();

// iterate over all the content nodes in the root
[].forEach.call(root.querySelectorAll('content'), function (contentNode) {
    // get the distributed nodes for each content node
    // and iterate over the distributed nodes
    [].forEach.call(contentNode.getDistributedNodes(),
        function (distributedNode) {
        // do something cool with the contentNode
    });
});

// Element.getDestinationInsertionPoints
var hostChildNode = document.querySelector('#some-host .some-child-node');

// get child node insertion points and iterate over them
[].forEach.call(hostChildNode.getDestinationInsertionPoints(),
    function (contentNode) {
    // do something cool with the contentNode
});
```

Shadow Insertion Points

In the previous section we examined how shadow host content can be projected into insertion points, <content>. Just as content can be projected into insertion points, so can shadow roots. Shadow root insertion points are defined using <shadow> tags. Like any other tags, these can be created directly in markup or added to the DOM programmatically.

 Shadow roots are stacked in the order they are added, with the youngest shadow root tree appearing last and rendering. Trees appearing earlier in the stack are referred to as *older trees*, while trees appearing after a given shadow root are referred to as *younger trees*.

At the beginning of this chapter it was stated that a shadow host could contain multiple shadow roots, but that only the last shadow root defined would be rendered. This is true in the absence of <shadow> elements. The <shadow> tag provides a point for projecting an older shadow root using a younger shadow root tree. If a shadow root tree contains more than one <shadow> element, the first one is used and the rest are ignored. Essentially, <shadow> allows you to render an older shadow root in a stack by providing an insertion point for it to be projected into.

 Projecting nodes to an insertion point does not affect the tree structure. The projected nodes remain in their original locations within the tree. They are simply displayed in the assigned insertion point.

Here's an example:

```
<template id="t-1">I am t1. </template>
<template id="t-2"><shadow></shadow>I am t2. </template>
<template id="t-3"><shadow></shadow>I am t3. </template>
<div id="root"></div>
<script type="text/javascript">
    (function () {
        var t1 = document.querySelector('#t-1');
        var t2 = document.querySelector('#t-2');
        var t3 = document.querySelector('#t-3');
        var host = document.querySelector('#root')
        var r1 = host.createShadowRoot();
        var r2 = host.createShadowRoot();
        var r3 = host.createShadowRoot();

        r1.appendChild(t1.content);
        r2.appendChild(t2.content);
        r3.appendChild(t3.content);
    })();
</script>
<!-- renders: "I am t1. I am t2. I am t3." -->
```

The previous code block renders from the bottom (youngest tree) up, projecting the next-oldest shadow root tree into the <shadow> insertion point. This was a very simple example. In a real application, the code will be more complicated and dynamic. Because of this it is helpful to have a way to inspect a <shadow> programmatically or to determine a shadow host's root:

```
// using the previous code block as an example
// determine older shadow root
r1.olderShadowRoot === null; // true; first in the stack
r2.olderShadowRoot === r1; // true
r3.olderShadowRoot === r2; // true
```

```
// determine a host's shadow root
host.shadowRoot === r1; // false; there can only be one (LIFO)
host.shadowRoot === r2; // false; ditto
host.shadowRoot === r3; // true

// determine a shadow root's host
r1.host === host; // true
r2.host === host; // true
r3.host === host; // true
```

Events and the Shadow DOM

At this point you might be thinking that projecting nodes instead of cloning them is a great optimization that will help to keep changes synchronized—but what about events bound to these projected nodes? How exactly does this work if they are not copied? In order to normalize these events, they are sometimes retargeted (*http://bit.ly/dwc-shadow-dom*) to appear as if they were triggered by the host element rather than the projected element in the shadow root. In these cases you can still determine the shadow root of the projected node by examining the `path` property of the event object. Some events are never retargeted, though, which makes sense if you think about it. For instance, how would a `scroll` event be retargeted? If a user scrolls one projected node, should the others scroll? The events that are not retargeted are:

- `abort`
- `error`
- `select`
- `change`
- `load`
- `reset`
- `resize`
- `scroll`
- `selectstart`

Updating the Dialog Template to Use the Shadow DOM

You might have noticed generic `id` values such as `title` and `content` were used in the dialog component, and you probably thought, "This idiot is going to have duplicate `id` values, which are supposed to be unique in the DOM, colliding left and right…" This was intentional, though, and has been leading up to this moment!

One of the benefits of the shadow DOM is the encapsulation of markup, which means the encapsulation of id values and a decrease in the likelihood of id value collisions in your application.

This code will leverage the previous chapter's code that demonstrated using a template to make the dialog component markup and JavaScript inert until it was appended to the DOM.

Dialog Markup

The dialog component will utilize a template, like the previous example, but this template will be appended to a shadow root that is hosted by `<div id="dialog-host">`. The interesting part about this example is that it is practically the reverse of our review widget example in terms of accessibility and readability. The aria (*http://bit.ly/dwc-aria*) attributes are contained within the shadow DOM, and the markup a developer writes is not exactly semantic. However, if you think about it, the aria attributes are primarily used for accessibility implementation details, so it makes sense that these details are obfuscated from the developer. The part that does not make sense is that the host markup is not very semantic, but please reserve judgment on that until the next chapter!

Here's the code for our updated dialog template:

```
<head>
    <script type="text/javascript" src="/vendor/jquery.js"></script>
    <template id="dialog">
        <style>
            // styling src
        </style>
        <script type="text/javascript">
            // dialog component source
        </script>
        <div role="dialog" aria-labelledby="title" aria-describedby="content">
            <h2 id="title"></h2>
            <p id="content"></p>
        </div>
    </template>
</head>
<!-- example host node -->
<div id="dialog-host">
    <h2>I am a title</h2>
    <p>Look at me! I am content.</p>
</div>
```

Dialog API

If you want to encapsulate the creation of the shadow root, the cloning and appending of the template, and the dialog component instantiation, then it is best to create a wrapper constructor function that encapsulates all of these implementation details:

```
function DialogShadow(options) {
    this.options = options;
    // get the host node using the hostQrySelector option
    this.host = document.querySelector(options.hostQrySelector);
    // grab the template
    this.template = document.querySelector('#dialog');
    this.root = this.host.createShadowRoot();
    // append the template content to the root
    this.root.appendChild(this.template.content);
    // get a reference to the dialog container element in the root
    this.el = this.root.querySelector('[role="dialog"]');

    this.options.$el = this.el;
    // align element to body since it is a fragment
    this.options.alignToEl = document.body;
    this.options.align = 'M';
    // do not clone node
    this.options.clone = false;

    // get the content from the host node; projecting would retain host
    // node styles and not allow for encapsulation of template styles
    this.el.querySelector('#title').innerHTML = this.host.querySelector('h2')
        .innerHTML;
    this.el.querySelector('#content').innerHTML = this.host.querySelector('p')
        .innerHTML;

    // create a dialog component instance
    this.api = new Dialog(this.options);

    return this;
}
```

Updating the Dialog show Method

Since the shadow root and its children are a subtree that is not part of the parent document, we have to ensure that the host element's z-index value is modified so that it appears on the top of its stacking context, the <body>:

```
// see GitHub repo for full example
(function (window, $, Voltron, Duvet, Shamen, ApacheChief, jenga) {

    'use strict';

    // makes dialog visible in the UI
    Dialog.prototype.show = function () {
```

```
        // this will adjust the z-index, set the display property,
        // and position the dialog
        this.overlay.position();
        // bring the host element to the top of the stack
        jenga.bringToFront(this.$el[0].parentNode.host);
    };

})(window, jQuery, Voltron, Duvet, Shamen, ApacheChief, jenga);
```

Instantiating a Dialog Component Instance

The dialog component can now be instantiated just as before, but it will now be scoped to the shadow root:

```
var dialog = new DialogShadow({
    draggable: true,
    resizable: true,
    hostQrySelector: '#dialog-host'
});

dialog.api.show();
```

Summary

In this chapter we introduced the shadow DOM and discussed the primary benefit it affords developers: encapsulation. Before the shadow DOM, the only way to achieve this level of encapsulation was to use an <iframe>. We then discussed, in great detail, the encapsulation of styling, including the new supporting CSS selectors and the rationale for these new selectors. We then covered the projection of nodes to insertion points, using <content> and <shadow> elements. This included the usage of the new select attribute for selecting specific content from a host node. Next, we examined the properties and methods for inspecting distributed, host, and root nodes. After that, we highlighted how events work in host and root nodes. Finally, we updated the dialog component example to use a shadow DOM.

Creating Custom Elements

Jason Strimpel

Raise your hand if you have seen markup like this:

```
<ul class="product-listing">
    <li class="product">
        <img src="img/log.jpg" alt="log" />
        <h3>log</h3>
        <p>
            What rolls down stairs<br />
            alone or in pairs,<br />
            and over your neighbor's dog?<br />
            What's great for a snack,<br />
            And fits on your back?<br />
            It's log, log, log<br />
        <p>
        <ul class="reviews">
            <li class="review">
                <div class="reviewer">
                    <img src="img/rcrumb.jpg" alt="R. Crumb" />
                    <div class="reviewer-name">R. Crumb</div>
                </div>
                <p>
                    We are living surrounded by illusion, by professionally
                    created fairy tales. We barely have contact with the real
                    world.
                </p>
            </li>
        </ul>
    </li>
</ul>
```

This markup is fairly semantic, and you can easily determine its intent. However, what if you could make it even more semantic and easier to understand? Consider this version:

```
<product-listing>
    <product-desc name="log" img="img/log.jpg">
        What rolls down stairs<br />
        alone or in pairs,<br />
        and over your neighbor's dog?<br />
        What's great for a snack,<br />
        And fits on your back?<br />
        It's log, log, log<br />
        <product-reviews>
            <product-review>
                <product-reviewer name="R. Crumb" img="img/rcrumb.jpg" />
                We are living surrounded by illusion, by professionally
                created fairy tales. We barely have contact with the real
                world.
            </product-review>
        </product-reviews>
    </product-desc>
</product-listing>
```

All the extraneous markup and properties have been eliminated, making it under-
standable at a glance. Until recently, this second version would not have been possible. What makes it possible today are *custom elements* (*http://bit.ly/dwc-custom*).

Introducing Custom Elements

The intent of custom elements is to provide a common way to encapsulate functionality in a self-describing manner that can be reused. Additionally, this mechanism
provides a consistent life cycle for elements, and an API for registering and extending
elements.

In order to leverage custom elements, you must first determine if the browser rendering the page supports them:

```
// determine if browser supports custom elements
var supportsCustomElements = (function () {
    return 'registerElement' in document;
})();
```

Registering Custom Elements

In order for a browser to recognize and support a custom element, it must first be
registered with the browser. This is done via document.registerElement, which
takes two arguments. The first argument is the name of the custom element being
registered. The second argument is an options object, which allows you to define the
prototype from which the element inherits. The default prototype is
HTMLElement.prototype. This options argument also provides a mechanism for
extending native elements, which will be covered in the next section of this chapter.

You register an element as follows:

```
// register an element
document.registerElement('product-listing');

// reigster an element and specify the prototype option
document.registerElement('product-listing', {
    prototype: Object.create(HTMLElement.prototype)
});
```

 Registering a custom element adds the element to the browser's registry (*http://bit.ly/dwc-registry*). This registry is used for resolving elements to their definitions.

Once a custom element has been registered, it can be referenced and utilized like a native element:

```
// create an instance of the product-listing custom element
var productListingEl = document.createElement('product-listing');
// append it to the DOM
document.body.appendChild(productListingEl);
```

Naming Conventions

You might have noticed that the name of our example custom element was all lower-case, and contained a dash (-). This is per the W3C specification (*http://bit.ly/dwc-concepts*). The rationale behind the naming convention is to prevent name collisions from occurring as new elements are added to the HTML specification and to allow browsers to easily distinguish custom elements from native elements.

Extending Elements

document.registerElement provides a method for extending both custom elements and native elements via the options argument.

Extending Custom Elements

Custom elements can be extended by adding the extends property to the document.registerElement options object in addition to specifying the prototype:

```
// create a custom element that represents a turtle
var Turtle = document.registerElement('regular-turtle');

// extend regular-turtle custom element
var NinjaTurtle = document.registerElement('ninja-turtle', {
    prototype: Object.create(turtle.prototype, {
        isMutant: { value: true },
```

```
    isNinja: { value: true }
  }),
  extends: 'regular-turtle'
});
```

These extended custom elements and their bases can then be instantiated in three different ways:

```
// declared in markup
<regular-turtle></regular-turtle>
<ninja-turtle></ninja-turtle>

// document.createElement
var regularTurtle = document.createElement('regular-turtle');
var ninjaTurtle = document.createElement('ninja-turtle');

// new operator
var regularTurtle = new Turtle();
var ninjaTurtle = new NinjaTurtle();
```

Extending Native Elements

Native elements can be extended in the same fashion as custom elements:

```
var fancyTable = document.registerElement('fancy-table', {
  prototype: Object.create(HTMLTableElement.prototype),
  extends: 'table'
});
```

When a native element is extended by a custom element it is referred to as a *type extension custom element*. The difference between extending custom elements and native elements is that native elements have the added benefit of declaratively defining themselves as being enhanced versions of their native counterparts. For example, this HTML declaration is stating that <table> is a type of fancy-table:

```
<table is="fancy-table"></table>
```

Defining Properties and Methods

This is where the fun begins! Just as native elements have properties (e.g., parentNode and methods (e.g., cloneNode), custom elements can define their own. This allows a developer to create a public API for a custom element.

The process for adding properties to an element prototype is not any different than doing so for other object prototypes. We have already seen one example that uses Object.create to define all the properties at once, but the following code block illustrates some different methods:

```
// better like this?
Turtle.prototype.walk = function () {
  // walk this way
```

```
};

// or better like this?
Object.defineProperty(NinjaTurtle.prototype, 'fight', {
    value: function () {
        // hiya
    }
});

// better like this?
Turtle.prototype.legs = 4;
```

Resolving Custom Elements

If you have experimented with creating elements that are not defined by one of
the HTML specifications—e.g., <jason-is-awesome>—then you know that a browser's HTML parser will happily accept such an element and continue processing the
document without hesitation. This is because the browser resolves the element to
HTMLUnknownElement (*http://bit.ly/dwc-htmlunknown*). All elements of unknown type
and deprecated elements (remember <blink>?) inherit from this type. The same is
true for custom elements that have yet to be registered. For instance, <jason-is-
awesome> could be declared in the markup and then registered after the fact:

```
<body>
    <jason-is-awesome>Let me count the ways.</jason-is-awesome>
    <script type="text/javascript">
        var jasonIsAwesomeEl = document.querySelector('jason-is-awesome');
        // isUnknown is true
        var isUnknown = jasonIsAwesomeEl.__proto__ === HTMLUnknownElement
            .prototype;

        document.registerElement('jason-is-awesome');
        // isUnknown is false
        isUnknown = jasonIsAwesomeEl.__proto__ === HTMLUnknownElement.prototype;
    </script>
</body>
```

If a custom element's prototype is no longer an HTMLUnknownElement.prototype
once it has been registered, then what is it? In this case it is an HTMLElement.proto
type, because that is the default prototype:

```
// continuing from the last example...
// isHTMLElement is true
var isHTMLElement = jasonIsAwesomeEl.__proto__ === HTMLElement.prototype;
```

Hooking Into Custom Element Life Cycles

One feature that JavaScript widgets lack is a clearly defined life cycle. Libraries such as
YUI have done a great job of defining a life cycle (*http://bit.ly/dwc-yui*) for their base

class widgets. However, there is not a standardized widget life cycle across libraries. In my opinion as an application and framework developer, this is one of the greatest benefits that custom elements offer.

I cannot count how many times I have encountered life cycle issues combining different widgets and widget libraries. You spend all your time either attempting to wrap them in a common life cycle or applying miscellaneous patches until your application becomes completely unmanageable. Custom elements are not the panacea for life cycle issues, but they at least provide a standardized set of hook points into an element's life cycle. If they provided too much structure, then they would be extremely inflexible and likely make a fair amount of assumptions that turned out to be incorrect.

Fortunately, custom elements have hook points at specific times in their life cycles that help provide consistency in terms of when and how your code executes:

createdCallback

createdCallback is called when an instance of the element is created:

```
var CallbackExample = document.registerElement('callback-example');
CallbackExample.prototype.createdCallback = function () {
    alert('and boom goes the dynomite');
}

// createdCallback is executed
document.createElement('callback-example');
```

attachedCallback

attachedCallback is called when an element is attached to the DOM:

```
var CallbackExample = document.registerElement('callback-example');
CallbackExample.prototype.attachedCallback = function () {
    alert('Put yourself in my position.');
}
var cbExampleEl = document.createElement('callback-example');

// attachedCallback is executed
document.body.appendChild(cbExampleEl);
```

detachedCallback

detachedCallback is called when an element is removed from the DOM:

```
var CallbackExample = document.registerElement('callback-example');
CallbackExample.prototype.detachedCallback = function () {
    alert('He died, too. So it goes.');
}
var cbExampleEl = document.createElement('callback-example');
```

```
document.body.appendChild(cbExampleEl);
// detachedCallback is executed
document.body.removeChild(cbExampleEl);
```

attributeChangedCallback

attributeChangedCallback is called when an element attribute has changed. The callback is passed three arguments—the attribute name, previous attribute value, and new attribute value:

```
<head>
    <script type="text/javascript">
        var CallbackExample = document.registerElement('callback-example');
        CallbackExample.prototype
            .attributeChangedCallback = function (attr, prevVal, newVal) {
            alert('Change places!');
        }
    </script>
</head>
<body>
    <callback-example change-places="fry" />
    <script type="text/javascript">
        var cbExampleEl = document.querySelector('callback-example');

        // attributeChangedCallback is executed
        cbExampleEl.setAttribute('change-places', 'bender');
    </script>
</body>
```

Styling Custom Elements

Styling a custom element is no different from styling any other element:

```
/* type extension attribute selector */
[is="four-roses"] {
    color: Brown;
    opacity: 0.5;
}

/* custom element tag name */
sculpin-ipa {
    color: GoldenRod
    opacity: 0.4;
}
```

The only difference is that a new pseudoselector, :unresolved, now exists to help prevent FOUCs (flashes of unstyled content) for custom elements that have not been registered when the DOM is being parsed and rendered.

This occurs because the custom element will not be rendered until its definition is resolved by the browser. In some cases this may not matter because the element registration will occur before rendering, as with a nondeferred <script> in the <head>, but in other cases registration will occur after rendering, as in the case of a <script> at the bottom of the <body>. In the latter case the custom element would render unstyled. Then, once the element had been registered, the styling would be applied and a repaint or redraw would occur, resulting in a FOUC. This is a good example use case for :unresolved. One preventative measure would be to set the opacity of the unresolved elements to 0:

```
[is="four-roses"]:unresolved {
    // nothing to see here
    opacity: 0;
}

sculpin-ipa:unresolved {
    // nothing to see here
    opacity: 0;
}
```

Utilizing Templates and the Shadow DOM with Custom Elements

One of the benefits of web components is that they are just sets of APIs that support the concept of making the Web a better development platform, so you can decide when and how you utilize them. In the case of custom elements it makes sense to store the element contents inside of a template, so they remain inert until an instance of the element is created. The shadow DOM is also useful in the case that you do not want the innards of your custom element exposed, to prevent potential issues if developers intentionally or accidentally manipulate the element's child nodes. The shadow DOM also provides the added benefit of style encapsulation so that none of the custom element styles bleed out and parent page styles do not bleed through.

The following example illustrates the use of a template and shadow DOM with a custom element:

```
<head>
    <template class="draag-children">
        <style>
            p span {
                text-decoration: underline;
            }
        </style>
        <p>
            <span>Draag child 1</span>: It doesn't move.
        </p>
```

```
        <p>
            <span>Draag child 2</span>: What a shame we can't play with her any
                more.
        </p>
    </template>
    <script type="text/javascript">
        document.registerElement('fantastic-planet', {
            prototype: Object.create(HTMLElement.prototype, {
                createdCallback: {
                    value: function () {
                        var template = document
                            .querySelector('.draag-children');

                        var content = document
                            .importNode(template.content, true);

                        // the context, this, is the custom element in
                        // element instance methods
                        this.createShadowRoot().appendChild(content);
                    }
                }
            })
        });
    </script>
</head>
<body>
    <fantastic-planet />
</body>
```

Converting the Dialog Component to a Custom Element

This is where the power of web components really begins to shine. The ability to encapsulate (and obfuscate) a UI component, such as a dialog, into a declarative interface, a custom element, is an extremely concise and powerful pattern. It frees the custom element implementer, to a certain degree, from the concern of maintaining backward compatibility with an extensive public API. It also allows the implementer to easily interchange implementation details and technologies in an inert template. Lastly, it protects the implementer and the consumer from runtime conflicts because of the encapsulation the shadow DOM offers.

 The sections that follow display the applicable portions of the registerElement prototype with the call for context. In reality these would all be part of the same prototype of a single registerElement call.

Creating the Dialog Custom Element

The first step in converting the dialog component to a custom element is to define the template and register the element (the life cycle callback will be implemented in a later section):

```
<head>
    <script type="text/javascript" src="/vendor/jquery.js"></script>
    <template id="dialog">
        <style>
            // styling source
        </style>
        <script type="text/javascript">
            // dialog component source
        </script>
        <div role="dialog" aria-labelledby="title" aria-describedby="content">
            <h2 id="title"></h2>
            <p id="content"></p>
        </div>
    </template>
    <script type="text/javascript">
        // callback will be implemented later
        document.registerElement('dialog-component', {
            prototype: Object.create(HTMLElement.prototype, {
                createdCallback: { value: function () {} }
            });
        });
    </script>
</head>
<body>
    <dialog-component title="Heavy Traffic">
        What makes you happy? What makes you happy? Where do you go? <br />
        Where do you go? Where do you hide? Where do you hide? <br />
        Who do you see? Who do you see? Who do you trust? <br />
        Who do you trust?
    </dialog-component>
</body>
```

Implementing the Dialog Custom Element's Callbacks

The injection and activation of the template contents should be done upon element creation. This ensures that the content will only be activated once per element:

```
// private and public properties and methods referenced in the callback
// will be defined in the next section
document.registerElement('dialog-component', {
    prototype: Object.create(HTMLElement.prototype, {
        createdCallback: {
            enumerable: false,
            value: function () {
                var template = document.querySelector('#dialog');
                var content = document.importNode(template.content, true);
```

```
                    var draggable = this.getAttribute('draggable');
                    var resizable = this.getAttribute('resizable');
                    var options = {
                        draggable:  draggable === undefined ? true : draggable,
                        resizable: resizable === undefined ? true : resizable,
                        hostQrySelector: this
                    };

                    this.root = this.createShadowRoot().appendChild(content);
                    // get a reference to the dialog container element in the root
                    this.dialogEl = this.root.querySelector('[role="dialog"]');
                    options.$el = this.dialogEl;
                    // align element to body since it is a fragment
                    options.alignToEl = document.body;
                    options.align = 'M';
                    // do not clone node
                    options.clone = false;

                    // get the content from the host node; projecting would retain
                    // host node styles and not allow for encapsulation of template
                    // styles
                    this.setTitle(this.host.getAttribute('title'));
                    this.setContent(this.innerHTML);

                    // create a dialog component instance
                    this.api = new Dialog(this.options);
                }
            }
        });
    });
```

Implementing the Dialog Custom Element API

The final step is creating an API. Some properties will be considered public and will be enumerable. Private properties will not be enumerable:

```
document.registerElement('dialog-component', {
    prototype: Object.create(HTMLElement.prototype, {
        // public
        show: {
            value: function () {
                this.api.show();
            },
            enumerable: true
        },
        hide: {
            value: function () {
                this.api.hide();
            },
            enumerable: true
        },
        setTitle: {
```

```
            value: function (title) {
                this.dialogEl.querySelector('#title').innerHTML = title;
            },
            enumerable: true
        },
        setContent: {
            value: function (content) {
                this.dialogEl.querySelector('#content').innerHTML = content;
            },
            enumerable: true
        },
        // private
        dialogEl: {},
        root: {},
        api: {}
    });
});
```

Showing the Dialog

Now that an API for the dialog custom element has defined, a developer can show it and set values:

```
// get a reference to the custom element
var dialog = document.querySelector('dialog-component');
// use the custom element's public API to show it
dialog.show();
```

Summary

In this chapter, we first introduced custom elements and outlined the primary benefits: maintainability, readability, encapsulation, etc. Next, we examined registering elements, extending custom and native elements, and adding properties and methods to elements, affording developers a way to extend the Web. Then we reviewed how the browser resolves elements. After that we looked at the custom element life cycle and the callbacks available for different points in the life cycle. We discussed how these callbacks help to create a consistent life cycle, which makes development, debugging, and maintenance easier. Next, we saw that native element styling rules apply to custom elements as well and introduced a new pseudoselector that helps to prevent FOUCs, a common problem with modern web applications. Then we saw the benefits of using templates and the shadow DOM in conjunction with custom elements. Finally, we applied these learnings to create a custom element for the dialog component, adding all the aforementioned benefits to our component.

CHAPTER 13

Importing Code

Jason Strimpel

Practically every other application platform allows packaging and importing code, but the web platform does not. This makes it extremely difficult to share code in a common fashion across applications. In the absence of a standard import, many other creative solutions have been invented and adopted by developers. However, none of these solutions have holistically addressed the need to include CSS, JavaScript, HTML, images, etc. as a single resource. This is what imports promise to deliver.

 There are imports already, in the sense that there are <link> tags for CSS and <script> tags for JavaScript that work for including code. However, these do not scale well or allow developers to define complete resources in a standard way that works consistently.

Declaring an Import

Importing code is as simple as adding a <link> and setting the rel value to *import*:

```
<head>
    <link id="meeseeks-import" rel="import" href="/imports/meeseeks/index.html">
</head>
```

Imports can also be added to a document programmatically:

```
<head>
    <script type="text/javascript">
        var link = document.createElement('link');
        link.rel = 'import';
        link.id = 'meeseeks-import';
        link.href = '/imports/meeseeks/index.html';
        link.onload = function (e) {
```

```
                // do something with import
        };
        link.onerror = function (e) {
            // doh! something went wrong loading import
            // handle error accordingly
        };

        document.head.appendChild(link);
    </script>
</head>
```

 An import is only loaded and parsed once, based on the URL, regardless of how many times it is requested, so the imported Java-Script is only executed once.

In order to make use of the resources in an import—CSS, HTML, and JavaScript—the browser must support imports. Detecting support for imports can be done by checking for the `import` property in a `<link>`:

```
// determine if browser supports imports
var supportsImports = (function () {
    return 'import' in document.createElement('link');
})();
```

Accessing an Import's Content

The content of an import can be accessed by getting a reference to the import `<link>` and accessing the `import` property. Let's use the source of the import referenced in the previous section, `/imports/meeseeks/index.html`, as an example:

```
<link rel="stylesheet" href="index.css" id="meeseeks-styles"></link>
<template id="meeseeks-template">
    <p>I'm Mr. Meeseeks, look at me!</p>
</template>
<script type="text/javascript">
    var MrMeeseeks = (function () {
        'use strict';

        // importer/parent document; more on this later
        var parentDocument = document;
        // import document; more on this later
        var importDocument = parentDocument.currentScript.ownerDocument;
        var template = importDocument.querySelector('#meeseeks-template')
            .content;

        function MrMeeseeks(el, options) {
            var self = this;
```

```
            this.options = options;
            this.el = el;
            // append template to parent el
            this.el.appendChild(parentDocument
                .importNode(template.content, true);
            // set interval to check if task has been completed
            this.isDoneInterval = setInterval(function () {
                self.isTaskComplete();
            }, this.interval);
        }

        MrMeeseeks.prototype.limit = 3600000;

        MrMeeseeks.prototype.interval = 60000;

        MrMeeseeks.prototype.taskComplete = false;

        MrMeeseeks.prototype.isTaskComplete = function () {
            if (this.taskComplete) {
                clearInterval(this.isDoneInterval);
                return;
            }

            alert('Existence is pain to a Meeseeks Jerry...' +
                'and we will do anything to alleviate that pain!');
        }

        return MrMeeseeks;
    })();
</script>
```

There is quite a bit of new material in the previous code block. Let's break it down section by section. The `MrMeeseeks` constructor is handling all the resources in this import, but the parent document that imported the code can just as easily access the code as well.

Referencing Documents

You might have noticed `parentDocument.currentScript.ownerDocument` at the top of the immediately invoked function wrapper inside of the /imports/meeseeks/ index.html import. `parentDocument` is a reference to document, which is the document that imported the import. document is always the top-level document, regardless of the context. The `currentScript` (*http://bit.ly/dwc-currentscript*) value is the "`<script>` element whose script is currently being processed," and `ownerDocument` (*http://bit.ly/dwc-nodeowner*) returns the top-level document object for a node. The combination of these two properties returns a reference to the import document.

An import document can be referenced from the main document by selecting the import node and accessing the `import` property:

```
var importDocument = document.querySelector('#meeseeks-import').import
```

Applying Styles

Styles are automatically applied to the main document when an import is loaded, so it is important to ensure that the import being loaded has properly namespaced its selectors. Styles can be removed by deleting the import node or by targeting `<link>` and `<style>` nodes in the import:

```
// remove the import
var link = document.querySelector('#meeseeks-import');
link.parentNode.removeChild(link);

// remove an import link node
var importDocument = document.querySelector('#meeseeks-import').import
var importLink = importDocument.querySelector('#meeseeks-styles');
importLink.parentNode.removeChild(importLink);
```

 If an import `<link>` with the same URL as a previously added import is added to the main document, it does not impact the CSS cascade. However, if an import `<link>` is removed from the main document and then an import `<link>` with the same URL as the removed import is added, it *does* impact the CSS cascade. The CSS cascade is also impacted if the import `<link>` nodes' order is programmatically modified in the DOM tree.

The latter example is probably not that useful, but there are a couple of different use cases that make the former example of removing imports from the main document worthwhile. One use case is if you are using imports to apply themes to an application and the application allows users to toggle between themes (e.g., Gmail). A second use case is if you have a single-page application that lazy loads resources on a per-route basis, which requires adding and removing resources as a user navigates throughout the application.

 In a single-page application (*http://bit.ly/dwc-spa*) (SPA), either all necessary code—HTML, JavaScript, and CSS—is retrieved with a single page load, or the appropriate resources are dynamically loaded and added to the page as necessary, usually in response to user actions. The page does not reload at any point in the process, nor does control transfer to another page, although modern web technologies (such as those included in HTML5) can provide the perception and navigability of separate logical pages in the application. Interaction with the SPA often involves dynamic communication with the web server behind the scenes.

The following example demonstrates the first use case, applying themes:

```
<!-- possible theme import examples to be loaded -->
<link data-theme="Stummies" rel="import" href="/imports/themes/stummies.html">
<link data-theme="GLeeMONEX" rel="import" href="/imports/themes/gleemonex.html">

// called on theme load
function onLoad(e) {
    var theme = this.dataset.theme;
    removeNodes('[data-theme]:not([data-theme="' + theme + '"])');
}

// called on theme load error
function onError(e) {
    var theme = this.dataset.theme;
    alert('Error loading the ' + theme + '!');
}

// used to remove previously loaded theme(s)
function removeNodes(selector) {
    var nodes = document.querySelectorAll(selector);

    [].forEach.call(nodes, function (node) {
        node.parentNode.removeChild(node);
    });
}

// called when user has selected a new theme in the UI
function setTheme(theme) {
    var link = document.createElement('link');

    link.rel = 'import';
    link.dataset.theme = theme;
    link.href = '/imports/themes/' + theme.toLowerCase() + '.html';
    link.onload = onLoad;
    link.onerror = onError;

    document.head.appendChild(link);
}
```

Accessing Templates

An import is an excellent mechanism for loading templates in the main document.
Import templates can be accessed just like <link> nodes:

```
var importDocument = document.querySelector('#meeseeks-import').import;
var template = importDocument.querySelector('#meeseeks-template');
var templateClone = document.importNode(template.content, true);

document.querySelector('body').appendChild(templateClone);
```

One use case for importing templates is loading a commonly used set of templates, such as error pages that could be used by every route in a single-page application. For instance, if a route cannot locate a resource such as a controller object or there is an error loading the model data for the route, then it might be appropriate to respond with a 404-template or 500-template error:

```
<!-- import template content error -->
<template id="500-template">Something went terribly wrong.</template>
<template id="404-template">We can't find it.</template>

function onError(code, target) {
    var errorDocument = document.querySelector('#errors-import').import;
    var template = errorDocument.querySelector('#' + code + '-template');
    var templateClone = document.importNode(template.content, true);

    target.appendChild(templateClone);
}
```

Executing JavaScript

JavaScript in an import is executed in the context of the main document, window.document. This is important because it means that any variables or functions defined within a <script> in an import, outside of a closure, will be part of the global context, window. This is useful for exporting functions to the main document, but at the same time it creates the potential for global name collisions, so use it with care!

 Removing an import <link> from the main document does not remove the JavaScript that was executed by the import—keep this in mind when loading imports.

Understanding Imports in Relation to the Main Document

It is important to remember that basic best practices still apply when dealing with imports—minimize network calls, minify files, place scripts at the bottom of the page, etc. In addition to performance considerations, though, there are other aspects that need to be understood when importing documents.

Parsing Imports

Imports do not block the parsing of the main document, which means that all import scripts are processed as if they had the defer property set. Import scripts are processed in order after the main document has finished executing any JavaScript in its <script> nodes and external JavaScript that is not marked as deferred. This non-blocking behavior is beneficial because it means imports can be placed at the top of the `<head>`, allowing the browser to begin downloading and processing the content as soon as possible without impacting the loading and rendering of the main document As a consequence, all performance best practices for improving the rendering time of a page—e.g., placing `<script>` nodes at the bottom—still hold true.

Cross-Domain Considerations

Import URLs are governed by the same rules as AJAX requests, so cross-origin requests are not allowed unless the server that is responsible for delivering the imports has been configured to support cross-origin resource sharing (CORS) (*http://bit.ly/dwc-cors*). These restrictions should be taken into consideration when configuring a server that will be used as an import repository for serving applications on different domains.

Subimports

Imports can import other imports. The rationales for this are the same as for modularizing other code: reuse, abstractions, testability, extendibility, etc. The same parsing and execution rules apply.

Loading Custom Elements

Up to this point we have evaluated imports for loading CSS, templates, and Java-Script, and have explored ways for accessing and managing these resources. Throughout the examples the onus has been on the parent document to leverage these resources. The `MrMeeseeks` import example managed some of the resources through an API it exposed. This API made the management of resources easier and limited the exposure of implementation details. However, it attached the `MrMeeseeks` object to `window`, which violates a JavaScript best practice: do not pollute the global namespace. In a small application this is less of a problem, but the larger an application becomes the more likely there is to be a name collision in `window`, which could cause an application error. In order to properly manage this, a registration system and a contract between the import and the main document would need to be defined. Fortunately, web components make this possible for us via custom elements:

```
<style>
    sea-of-green:unresolved {
        opacity: 0;
    }

    sea-of-green {
        opacity: 1;
        background: green;
        border-radius: 50%
```

```
        }
    </style>
    <template id="sea-of-green">
        Hydrolate, verdant chrysoidine.
    </template>
    <script type="text/javascript">
        document.registerElement('sea-of-green', {
            prototype: Object.create(HTMLElement.prototype, {
                createdCallback: {
                    value: function () {
                        var template = document.querySelector('#sea-of-green');
                        var content = document.importNode(template.content, true);

                        this.createShadowRoot().appendChild(content);
                    }
                }
            })
        });
    </script>
```

The import loads a custom element that is self-registering because the JavaScript is executed after the import content and the main document have been parsed. This makes the custom element available to the main document automatically. In addition to this, the custom element provides a commonly understood contract because it has a natively defined life cycle. This custom element can then easily be used in the main document:

```
<head>
    <link rel="import" href="/imports/sea-of-green/index.html">
</head>
<body>
    <sea-of-green />
</body>
```

Importing the Dialog

Including the dialog custom element source in an import is simply a matter of copying and pasting the source into an import file. Then any page that includes the import can easily use the dialog custom element:

```
<head>
    <link rel="import" href="/imports/dialog/index.html">
</head>
<body>
    <dialog-component title="After Ford">
        Ending is better than mending. <br />
        The more stitches, the less riches.
    </dialog-component>
</body>
```

Summary

In this chapter we first introduced the premise for imports, then covered how to declare an import both programmatically and declaratively. Next we examined how to access an import's content, which included referencing the import and main documents, accessing styles, leveraging templates, and understanding JavaScript execution in an import. After that we looked at how imports are processed by the main document. Then we covered using imports to load custom elements and the benefits that the self-registering pattern offers. Finally, we saw how to use imports to load the dialog custom element into the main document.

PART IV

Testing, Building, and Deploying Components with Polymer

In Part III we went over the core of web components and their constituent technologies, gaining an understanding of the complexity that they present. In Part IV we will be porting our web component to take advantage of the Polymer framework, incorporating it into a Grunt build process, packaging it with Vulcanize, and publishing it with Bower. We'll also take a look at some of the currently available options for testing web components and show the end-to-end process of writing and running unit tests using Karma.

The Polymer Project is more than just a pleasing API for web components. It provides many, many shims that bring the future of web development to most relatively modern browsers today. Technologies like the shadow DOM aren't the easiest to polyfill, but the community has rallied around this suite of shims in order to provide consistent behavior across all modern browsers and in all competing frameworks. This means that you can feel relatively confident investing time in understanding Polymer, what its developers are trying to do, and how they are doing it even if you have not fully bought into the API.

As your projects grow and your usage of Polymerized web components increases, you'll soon find that managing web component source files requires a different level of concern than traditional development. You'll be managing multiple JavaScript, HTML, and CSS resources that can't be concatenated blindly with others of their kind. Gone are the days of treating JavaScript as an afterthought, and it is important to consider your source code as first class, having its own build process, pipeline, unit tests, linters, and analytics. Committing to a build tool like Grunt or Gulp early will allow you to manage these disparate tools, creating a task chain with a smooth flow and resulting in fewer headaches and less maintenance frustration. Vulcanize, a project created and maintained by the Polymer group, will help you package your web components for deployment or distribution. Finally, we'll cover publishing with Bower, an excellent tool for development that also provides an intuitive and standard way for users of your libraries to install them and get started quickly.

CHAPTER 14

Introducing Polymer

Jarrod Overson

There are a number of caveats to the use of web components as they stand today, but there are lots of people from lots of companies doing their best to help get you started as quickly as possible. Polymer is one such project that has gained traction quickly and has proven itself to be invaluable in the web component revolution. Polymer is a BSD-licensed suite of libraries that enable you to be productive with web components immediately.

Polymer Mission Statement

The expressed focus of Polymer is to "embrace HTML as much as possible by encouraging the use of custom elements wherever possible."

To help speed the adoption of future web technology, Polymer's authors have created shims for all related aspects of web components and tangential technologies. These shims are entirely usable outside of Polymer and are accepted as standard shims by companies like Mozilla and Microsoft, who use them with their own web component frameworks.

Considering that it is such a bleeding-edge technology, the Polymer group has done excellent work easing the transition to web component adoption. Polymer (outside of the Polymer elements) consists of two distinct layers of code. In this respect it is similar to jQuery, which is made up of jQuery itself and Sizzle. Sizzle is the independent selector engine that normalizes DOM selection for browsers that don't support get QuerySelector and similar methods. Most people aren't even aware of this abstraction because it's largely invisible to the end user.

Polymer proper is the opinionated sugar on top of standard APIs that provides a satisfying framework for creating and managing web components. The second, lower layer of code, known as *platform.js* (soon to be known as *webcomponents.js*), is an extensive series of shims that iron out APIs and inconsistencies across evergreen browsers.

Evergreens

"Evergreen" is the term adopted for AAA browsers that keep themselves up to date without user interaction. This includes every version of Chrome, modern Firefox, modern Opera, and IE 10+.

This is *not* a term used to denote browsers that support any particular technology and, as such, can be misleading when used to describe support. Unless browsers start deviating dramatically from specifications, it can be thought of as a term that means "a browser that will probably support emerging technologies in a reasonable time frame."

Figure 14-1 shows the Polymer group's explanation of its component pieces. You can see the distinct layers that make up the Polymer framework and the foundational pieces that make up the platform.

The long-term goal of Polymer, with respect to its platform shims, is to eventually reduce and eliminate the need for them completely. In its heyday, jQuery (like many other libraries) was required to support very old browsers, due to the time between version upgrades. Over the years this added up to a substantial amount of code that has been and will be around for a long time. Polymer's commitment to only supporting evergreen browsers ensures that the gradual removal of shim code is likely to be a reality, albeit at the substantial cost of limited browser support. Internet Explorer's support starts at version 10, and Safari's support doesn't extend to versions before Safari 6. There are other community shims that provide limited support to earlier browsers, but that is beyond the scope of Polymer and this book.

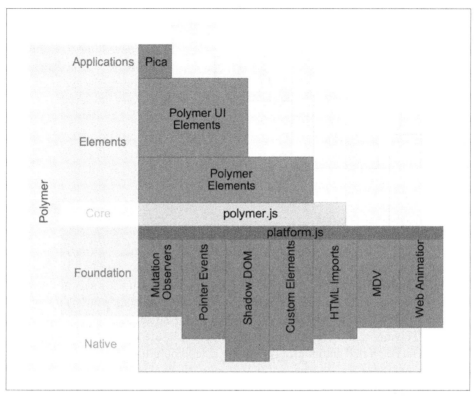

Figure 14-1. Polymer components (source: https://www.polymer-project.org)

Polymer Versions

This book was conceived during the Polymer 0.1 era (the "alpha" years), started taking form while Polymer 0.2 was in use, and matured to completion as Polymer evolved to version 0.8. Polymer 0.8 is still in preview on a branch on GitHub at the time of this book's publication. The jump from 0.5 to 0.8 saw some major changes to the Polymer philosophy, but the majority of those choices don't affect the common usage of Polymer. Polymer 0.8 focuses on performance and cutting out features that, ultimately, people weren't using. The functionality still exists in add-on libraries but has been removed from the core Polymer builds.

Since the changes in 0.8 (at the time of publication) don't substantially affect the ideas in this book, and given that the Polymer team is still making decisions as to what Polymer 0.8 (and Polymer 1.0) will look like, the book's code is tailored around the 0.5 release.

Polymer's syntax was inspired by the <element> element, which is currently in spec limbo (*http://bit.ly/dwc-speclimbo*). This element was conceived as a way to declaratively define elements within an HTML document. It was removed due to complexities in its implementation but the fact that it can live on spiritually within Polymer is a testament to this shift in how the Web is evolving. As developers, we are being provided with the tools necessary to build pieces of the Web at a very low level.

Polymer Elements

A basic Polymer element definition looks like this:

```
<polymer-element name="hello-world" noscript>
  <template>
    <h1>Hello World</h1>
  </template>
</polymer-element>
```

The syntax should look reasonably intuitive, and if you've just read Part III, the simplicity is probably welcome. This small chunk of code defines a custom element called `hello-world` that, when instantiated, will clone the template's content and append it to the element's shadow root. The `noscript` attribute on `polymer-element` just tells Polymer that we're not doing any scripting inside the element and that the element can be created automatically with the default options.

Now contrast this to the steps you needed to take with bare web component APIs in Part II, and you might get that "Ohhh, neat" feeling you had when you first started working with jQuery. There's no doubt that the web component APIs can be a little cumbersome and unintuitive, *especially* when combined with each other, so the benefit of this sugar is immediately apparent.

One of the substantial gains Polymer provides beyond the syntactic sugar is its two-way data binding integrated into templates and the JavaScript API. This allows you to declaratively define template replacements that are bound to attributes and other changing properties. For example, the following code:

```
<polymer-element name="x-greeting" attributes="target">
  <template>
    <h1>Hello {{target}}</h1>
  </template>
  <script>
    Polymer('x-greeting', {
      target: "World"
    });
  </script>
</polymer-element>
```

creates the x-greeting element, whose target attribute can be used to specify who should be greeted (defaulting to World):

```
<x-greeting target=Mom></x-greeting>
```

 Given the requirement that a custom element must have a hyphen in its name (see the sidebar "Naming Conventions" on page 129), a common practice is to namespace custom elements, as in polymer-tabs or myapp-button. In the case of reusable elements that don't exist in a logical namespace, a growing standard is to use the x- or sometimes ui- prefix for the element names.

For some elements, such as this one, it may be more intuitive to make use of the content of a custom element instead of an attribute. This can easily be done with the <content> tag:

```
<polymer-element name="x-greeting" noscript>
  <template>
    <h1>Hello <content>World</content></h1>
  </template>
</polymer-element>
```

Here we default our content to World again, but we can change who is greeted by specifying different content in the custom element instead of using an attribute:

```
<x-greeting>World!</x-greeting>
```

Notice we went back to using noscript in the preceding code sample; this isn't required to use <content>, but it's a good exercise to see just how complex we can make a custom element without requiring any scripting whatsoever. This is more important than it may seem—this is not an exercise for curiosity's sake. When you're playing with web components you are implicitly defining your environment as being close to or beyond the leading edge. This provides you with a wide array of CSS styles, animations, and techniques that most people probably aren't familiar with, due to common browser compatibility requirements. It's important to reset your baseline in order to make the most out of web components.

Resetting Your Baseline

It's not only CSS that you may need to brush up on. Technologies like SPDY (*http://bit.ly/dwc-spdy*) now become something you can reliably invest in, and SPDY itself is more than just a "faster Web." SPDY dramatically reduces the cost of serving many small files from the same server. This will have substantial implications for how web sources are structured, maintained, and built in the future.

AMD or ES6 modules will not need to be concatenated together. HTML imports will not only be a viable solution, they will be the preferred abstraction layer, and sprite-sheets may be a thing of the past.

In this weird, alien future, even using a content delivery network may adversely affect perceived performance. Crazy, I know.

Adding Style

To start adding CSS rules to your elements, you simply add a `<style>` block to the `<template>`. We can use Polymer templates in CSS styles as well, allowing us to create dynamic styles with little extra effort.

Since we're in control of our own elements now, let's resurrect an old favorite, the `<font>` tag. Deprecation be damned!

```
<polymer-element name="x-font" attributes="color" noscript>
  <template>
    <style>
      span {
        color:{{color}};
      }
    </style>
    <span><content></content></span>
  </template>
</polymer-element>

<x-font color=red>Hello World!</x-font>
```

There's an important subtlety in the preceding code; did you spot it? If you don't specify a `color` attribute, what happens? It's probably an easy guess that the color of the resulting element is the inherited text color of the context the element is used in, but why? We actually get a "broken" CSS rule specifying that the color is `"null"`. This, conveniently, isn't a useful color, so the CSS engine just ignores it, but it's important to call out because web components should act like normal elements—and that means *silent errors and obvious fallbacks.*

There's a second important thing to note about our element. What do you think would happen if you did this?

```
<x-font color="red;font-style:italic">Hello World!</x-font>
```

Congratulations if you guessed that you'd get a red, italic "Hello World!" This isn't an artifact of web components—it's due to Polymer itself—but regardless of what you use to make web components, you're going to need to account for them being used in ways you don't expect. Maybe now we can all sit back and start to appreciate the jobs spec writers have been doing for the past few decades.

External Resources

As your web components grow in size, you'll need a way to better manage larger styles. Unfortunately, as we went over in Part III, you can't easily add external stylesheets via `<link>` tags to a shadow DOM. Fortunately, though, many smart people have traversed this path before us and have simplified some common use cases like this one. A template like the following wouldn't include any external styles when added to the shadow DOM manually:

```
<template>
    <link rel="stylesheet" href="styles.css">
    <span>Hello World</span>
</template>

span {
  font-style:italic;
}
```

In Polymer, though, that template would work perfectly fine and the styles would be applied to the elements in the shadow root (and the shadow root alone). How does that work? Polymer simply finds the `<link>` elements, asynchronously grabs the referenced CSS via an `XMLHttpRequest`, deletes the original `<link>` element, and inlines the CSS into a `<script>` tag at the location of the original link element. Simple, right? The resulting element in the DOM would look very similar to this:

```
<template>
    <style>
        span {
            font-style:italic;
        }
    </style>
    <link rel="stylesheet" href="styles.css">
    <span>Hello World</span>
</template>
```

Filtering Expressions

Polymer's templating additions also provide the ability to filter expressions through simple JavaScript functions. This provides a layer of abstraction between any advanced logic and the template itself, somewhat similar to the features provided by a lot of limited-logic templating solutions available for JavaScript right now. Let's add some classiness to our `x-font` tag by way of a `type` attribute where we can specify a predefined set of styles to apply:

```
<polymer-element name="x-font" attributes="type color" noscript>
  <template>
    <style>
      span {
        color:{{color}};
      }
```

```
      .shadow {
        text-shadow: 2px 2px 2px grey;
      }
    </style>
    <span class="{{ { shadow: type == 'fancy' } | tokenList }}">
      <content></content>
    </span>
  </template>
</polymer-element>
```

The block class="{{ {shadow: type == 'fancy'} | tokenList }}" probably
looks like it's doing a lot more than it really is. To isolate the important parts, we can
get rid of the attribute and wrapping quotes, class="", and the Polymer template
delimiters, {{ and }}. We're then left with { shadow: type == 'fancy' } | token
List, which we can further separate into two parts. The first part is a plain old Java-
Script object with one key, shadow, the value of which is the return value of the
comparison type == 'fancy'. The second part, | tokenList, is Polymer syntax that
pipes the lefthand side into the filter specified on the righthand side. tokenList is just
a plain JavaScript function located on the PolymerExpressions.prototype:

```
PolymerExpressions.prototype = {
    tokenList: function(value) {
        var tokens = [];
        for (var key in value) {
            if (value[key])
                tokens.push(key);
        }
        return tokens.join(' ');
    },
    [...]
}
```

Here we can see that the tokenList function takes in a JavaScript object and, for
every key, tests the truthiness of the key's value; it then adds the key name to an array
if it es. That array's values are then joined together, separated by a space (' '). We're
going through filters in depth here because they are very powerful and often over-
looked, and when you see them in a context like this one they are regularly seen as
more complicated than they really are. The filter in our Polymer template can be seen
as being equivalent to the following code:

```
var originalValue = {
    shadow: type == 'fancy' // 'type' is a defined attribute on our element
                            // e.g. <x-font type='fancy'></x-font>
};

var filteredValue = tokenList(originalValue);

// filteredValue === 'shadow'
```

Filters and data binding provide you with a substantial amount of control, without exposing much actual JavaScript. This is a great step toward creating maintainable applications and client code.

Template Syntax

We've already seen several examples of Polymer's template syntax, and there's a lot more going on with templates than we'll deal with here. More advanced expressions make use of attributes on nested `<template>` elements that provide common template functions like block repetition and conditional blocks.

Data Binding

Polymer offers intuitive data binding for anyone who has used Handlebars-style templates in other frameworks/templating solutions (i.e., where you bind a property of the context to a portion of a template by surrounding the identifier with double curly braces):

```
<polymer-element name="x-simple">
  <template>
    {{value}}
  </template>
  <script>
    Polymer('x-simple',{
      ready : function () {
        this.value = "Hello World!";
      }
    })
  </script>
</polymer-element>
```

Block Repetition

This approach combines the double curly brace style with HTML attributes in order to specify the behavior of subtree nodes, very similar to AngularJS-style template loops:

```
<polymer-element name="x-repeat">
  <template>
    <ul>
      <template repeat="{{ value in values }}">
        <li>{{value}}</li>
      </template>
    </ul>
  </template>
  <script>
    Polymer('x-repeat',{
      ready : function () {
        this.values = [1,2,3,4];
```

```
      }
    })
  </script>
</polymer-element>
```

Bound Scopes

Bound scopes are the template equivalent of JavaScript's with statement: they extend the scope chain of a subtree. They allow you to simplify references to extended properties without specifying redundant identifiers repeatedly:

```
<polymer-element name="x-bind">
  <template>
    <span>
      {{outerObject.outerValue}}
    </span>
    <template bind="{{outerObject.innerObject}}">
      <span>{{innerValue}}</span>
    </template>
  </template>
  <script>
    Polymer('x-bind',{
      ready : function () {
        this.outerObject = {
          outerValue : "Hello",
          innerObject : {
            innerValue : "World"
          }
        };
      }
    })
  </script>
</polymer-element>
```

Conditional Blocks

Polymer's conditional blocks follow the same style and are immediately intuitive:

```
<polymer-element name="x-editable">
  <template>
    <span>{{value}}</span>
    <template if="{{ !readonly }}">
        <input value="{{value}}">
    </template>
  </template>
  <script>
    Polymer('x-editable',{
      value : 'default',
      readonly : true
    })
  </script>
</polymer-element>
```

Multiple Template Directives at Once

An often underused aspect of template directives is the ability to combine items like `repeat` and `if`. Rather than nesting templates with their own directives, you can combine them in one template for a terser syntax:

```
<polymer-element name="x-combo">
  <template>
    <h1>A list of values</h1>
    <ul>
      <template repeat="{{ value in values }}" if="{{ open }}">
        <li>{{ value }}</li>
      </template>
    </ul>
  </template>
  <script>
    Polymer('x-combo',{
      values : [1,2,3,4],
      open : true
    })
  </script>
</polymer-element>
```

Attributes and Properties—Your Element's API

There is a lot to consider when determining how to construct and expose your custom element's API. When should something be an attribute? When should it be a property? Should it be both? How should it be bound? Should it be read-only? What should happen if it changes after instantiation? Should your element emit events? If so, what events? Should you model your element's API after an existing element or toss existing best practices aside?

There are other frameworks out there that do things strikingly similarly to what web components and Polymer provide, but web components exist on an isolated island far away from any application framework. The responsibility to create consistent, intuitive, and decidedly "HTML-like" APIs is important.

With Polymer you have the power to create a variety of API touchpoints that all have their own benefits and drawbacks.

Naked Attributes

As you'd probably expect, you can add any attribute you want to your custom element and access it via the standard `getAttribute` method that exists on instances of elements. You don't need to explicitly code this support, but it isn't bindable within templates, and Polymer doesn't offer you much sugar on top of it. You can add an attribute to your element as follows:

```
<polymer-element name="x-example" noscript>
</polymer-element>
<x-example attr="my attribute"></x-example>
<script>
  var myElement = document.querySelector('x-example');
  myElement.getAttribute('attr') == "my attribute"; // true
</script>
```

Published Properties

Polymer's "published properties" are probably what is going to get the most use in your custom elements. These properties are exposed versions of element attributes and are bindable within templates; when the attribute changes or the property changes, the templates will reflect this. Here's how to add a published property to your custom element:

```
<polymer-element name="x-example" noscript>
  <template>
    {{myAttribute}}
  </template>
</polymer-element>
<x-example myAttribute="hello world"></x-example>
<script>
  var myElement = document.querySelector('x-example');
  myElement.getAttribute('myAttribute'); // "hello world"
  myElement.myAttribute; // "hello world"
  myElement.setAttribute('myAttribute', 'til next time');
  myElement.myAttribute = 'later!';
</script>
```

Published properties are popular because they offer a lot of functionality in a simple package, and also because they are intuitive to users and are discoverable via Java-Script introspection and browser devtools.

Instance Methods

All methods applied to the prototype of the element within the Polymer definition are exposed as instance methods of the element within JavaScript:

```
<polymer-element name="x-example">
  <template>
    {{myAttribute}}
  </template>
  <script>
    Polymer('x-example', {
      myMethod : function(value) {
        this.myAttribute = value;
      }
```

```
    })
  </script>
</polymer-element>
<x-example myAttribute="hello world"></x-example>
<script>
  var myElement = document.querySelector('x-example');
  myElement.myMethod('howdy world');
</script>
```

This can be useful, but side effects should be kept to a minimum. Always keep in mind that you are notified when attributes have changed, so it may make more sense at an API level to have certain functionality triggered upon attribute change instead of via an instance method.

Polymer's JavaScript APIs

This chapter is nearly over, and we're only now touching on Polymer's JavaScript APIs. This is by design, because the beauty of web components, and the philosophy of Polymer, is to embrace HTML with all its modern power. HTML is no longer something you need to treat gently and twist and tweak to get where you want. You are defining the power of HTML. You'll be doing this with JavaScript, of course, but HTML is now sharing the front seat again.

Life Cycle Methods

The life cycle methods you are used to with custom elements are supported and easy to use within Polymer. For convenience, though, they are shorter than their spec equivalents. Polymer also adds other methods that align with important events in the Polymer life cycle. Table 14-1 lists these methods, and their spec equivalents (if any).

Table 14-1. Polymer life cycle methods

Polymer	Spec equivalent	Called when
created	createdCallback	The element has been created.
ready	None	Polymer has completed its initialization of the element.
attached	attachedCallback	The element has been attached to the DOM.
domReady	None	The initial set of children is guaranteed to exist.
detached	detachedCallback	The element has been detached from the page.
attributeChanged	attributeChangedCallback	An attribute has been added, removed, or changed.

Note and memorize the difference between `created` and `ready`. `created` simply marks that the element has been created and is an analog to `createdCallback` on naked custom elements; `ready` is called when Polymer has done its initialization work, injected the shadow DOM, set up listeners, and is largely ready to interact with. In a Polymer mindset, you'll likely always want to deal with the `ready` callback.

Events

You can emit events easily from your web component yourself, but for consistency in creation and usage, Polymer provides the `fire` method that automates this for you. The method's signature is intutive and expected, but it abstracts away common event boilerplate:

```
fire: function(type, detail, onNode, bubbles, cancelable) {
  var node = onNode || this;
  var detail = detail === null || detail === undefined ? {} : detail;
  var event = new CustomEvent(type, {
    bubbles: bubbles !== undefined ? bubbles : true,
    cancelable: cancelable !== undefined ? cancelable : true,
    detail: detail
  });
  node.dispatchEvent(event);
  return event;
}
```

Usage is straightforward, and you'll commonly only use the first one or two parameters (the event name and the data payload). The following example issues an *open* event with the target being the current context—which, in this example, would be the element itself:

```
this.fire('open', { target: this });
```

Managing Delayed Work

When you start encapsulating all work in components, you may find yourself commonly dealing with timeouts and the management thereof to ensure work is done only once and after a certain period of time. This could be for animations, notifications, event throttling... anything. It's so common that Polymer provides a common API for it, `.job`:

```
this.job('openDialog', function () {
  this.fire('open');
}, 100);
```

Summary

In this chapter we caught a glimpse of the future of the World Wide Web. It is important to note how the somewhat disparate technologies we looked at in Part III have been joined together by the community to offer a fairly pleasing API. This is a core philosophy touched on by the "Extensible Web Manifesto," a series of principles that seek to influence how web technology is standardized in the future.

Extensible Web Manifesto

- Focus on adding *new low-level capabilities* to the web platform that are secure and efficient.

- Expose low-level capabilities that *explain existing features*, such as HTML and CSS, allowing authors to understand and replicate them.

- Develop, describe, and test new high-level features in JavaScript, and allow web developers to iterate on them before they become standardized. This creates a *virtuous cycle* between standards and developers.

- *Prioritize efforts* that follow these recommendations and deprioritize and refocus those which do not.

This chapter outlined a large slice of what Polymer can do, and after reading it you should be able to create your own highly functional web components with ease. In the coming chapters we'll explore how to port our existing dialog to Polymer, test it, and build a distributable, installable package.

CHAPTER 15

Porting Our Dialog to Polymer

Jarrod Overson

There are 200 ways to write any one thing in browserland JavaScript, 400 ways of writing an encapsulated component, and 800 ways of porting any one component implemented within one framework to another.

We'll go over two such ways.

Web components provide a lot. They also introduce many questions, and each one of those questions can be answered differently depending on perspective, time constraints, and development attitude. Web components, at their base, provide a layer of abstraction and push an API touchpoint to the HTML itself. This is already a win, and for a lot of people, that is the primary appeal.

At the other extreme, there are people who see web components as an opportunity to implement the next generation of building blocks that will compose the Web of the future. There are already implementations of spec proposals floating around on the Internet, and it's not a stretch to believe that independently developed individual web components may end up as official elements existing in the actual HTML spec one day.

Neither attitude is necessarily better than the other; they are just different and excel in their own ways. With those two attitudes, though, comes a choice of tools and implementations. Do you reuse what you know, love, and are familiar with to get a job done? Or do you toss the past aside, and implement these building blocks from the ground up?

Why Port Anything to Polymer at All?

Why port anything to Polymer, or even use web components, at all? It's an extra burden and effort, for what gain? Those are questions we all should be asking ourselves when we incorporate any new technology into our existing workflows.

Libraries, frameworks, and tools hit their peak popularity after people recognize them as filling a need better than the tools around them. Once that need is filled and the best practices are understood, these offerings become the new baseline and developers start looking forward to new holes that need patching. As new libraries start from an existing baseline of experience and solutions, they provide extra value that old libraries may or may not compare to.

The libraries, patterns, and tools you use now will remain just as useful in the future, but they may or may not progress to take advantage of new practices that may start becoming standard. This can affect maintenance, hiring of new employees, and the speed at which new features can be developed.

The Progressive Web

Have you ever seen a JavaScript project managed by Ant? Or one built by Rhino? They exist, but you'd be hard pressed to find a popular project that deals with either of those technologies today.

Ant is still useful, as is Rhino, but they temporarily filled a gap that was better handled by tools that came later. Grunt and Node.js, by and large, have almost completely replaced Ant and Rhino in the JavaScript developer's toolbox.

What's next? Gulp became extremely popular very quickly because it leveraged a lot of the best ideas in Grunt, and iterated upon the ones that weren't so great.

What will come after Node.js? I don't know—there are projects attempting to bite off a piece of that pie, but it's far too early to tell what might stick. One such project is JXcore, a Node.js fork that handles multithreading and thread recovery and is seeking to provide a JavaScript-to-llvm solution.

The Web evolves quickly, and our websites and applications never "go gold" to be left and forgotten about. The ability to maintain and adapt is what separates successful web applications from their counterparts. There is always benefit in looking forward, keeping abreast of what is becoming popular and what is losing favor.

Getting comfortable is the Achilles' heel of software development, and doubly so for web development. If you seek to provide value and advance in your career, leaning toward the leading edge will pay off in spades. Getting set up with a web component flow now will help you going forward.

Web components are the future. There is tooling around them and there will be more, so a bet on them is one that will keep on paying out. They are not the *only* future, merely one rung in the ladder of progress—but it's a strong one that leads to a new, stable platform that we will spring off of again and again.

The Direct Port

It's relatively simple to do basic ports of your existing UI widgets to Polymer. You can reuse a lot of the logic for widgets written with libraries like jQuery, Backbone, or even Angular and Ember. This is part of the beauty of web components: they aren't introducing anything very new; they are offering you the opportunity to augment the old.

Managing Dependencies

You've already seen a lot of reusable code in this book so far, and it is probably starting to feel similar to code bases you have worked on yourself. There are very few ways to effectively manage JavaScript dependencies in browserland, and there are even fewer ways to manage third-party dependencies. The two major registries for browser based JavaScript are npm and Bower, both of which have very different ways of managing their packages.

While npm, the Node.js package manager, has become very effective for some people as a way to manage browser-based JavaScript, the methods of managing it are more tied to the Node world than to traditional browser development. We won't be covering npm-based browser code, but if you're interested, look into tools like Browserify and Webpack; they offer excellent solutions for a specific demographic.

 npm, Inc., the company formed to manage npm, recently posted on its blog (*http://bit.ly/dwc-npm-update*) the intent to "officially" support browser-based packages in the future. While we have no idea what that really means right now, it is a very appealing message and is worth keeping track of as an alternate solution in the future.

npm and its core developers have proven to be extremely adept at providing scalable, intuitive, and attractive dependency management solutions, so this is very good news.

Bower is a tool born out of Twitter specifically intended to manage browser-based JavaScript. There is, technically, a "registry," but it exists almost strictly as a URL-redirection service, mapping common names to destinations serving static files or Git repositories. Modules installed by Bower can specify a list of ignored files and dependencies, allowing you to automate the installation of many third-party files with one command.

One of the established patterns for reusable web components is to expect that all dependencies, components or otherwise, are flattened siblings in the immediate parent directory. This leaves a lot to be desired, but until something better comes along, it's the standard to abide by. This means that we can and should reference dependencies using relative paths, as siblings to the dependent module.

For example, we might reference an HTML file like this:

```
<link rel="import" href="../another_component/dependency.html">
```

and a script like this:

```
<script src="../jquery/jquery.js"></script>
<!--

Some component that is used by our original file.

-->
```

The dependency directory ends up looking a lot like this:

```
dependency_directory
|
|-- jquery
|    |-- jquery.js
|    |-- jquery.min.js
|    +-- jquery.js.map
|-- polymer
|    |-- polymer.js
|    |-- polymer.js.map
|    +-- polymer.html
+-- platform
     |-- platform.js
     +-- platform.js.map
```

Conveniently, (or likely because) Bower installs modules in this exact pattern, we can use it effectively to manage our web components and their dependencies. By default, Bower installs its packages in a *bower_components* directory, but this can be configured via a *.bowerrc* JSON file installed per project or in your home directory. For example, to use the vendor directory:

```
{
  "directory": "vendor"
}
```

For convenience and clarity, though, we'll continue to use *bower_components* here. That you are able to configure the directory is mentioned solely because that is very often the first question about the tool from people familiar with different development environments.

Installing Dependencies with Bower

Installing dependencies like Polymer with Bower is extremely easy, but first you need to have Node.js installed—it provides you with the runtime for the tools and with the package manager, npm, that is necessary to install another package manager, Bower. Node.js is installable in several different ways, all documented on the website (*http://nodejs.org*). To get Bower, you install it globally via npm:

```
$ npm install -g bower
```

On a standard install in a Linux-like environment like OS X or Ubuntu, you may need to sudo the command in order for it to install globally:

```
$ sudo npm install -g bower
```

Bower's basic usage is no different from nearly any other package manager: you simply issue an install command and then Bower will go out, find the destination for your package (often somewhere on GitHub), download and cache the files, parse the *bower.json* file for metadata, copy the listed files over to your destination directory, and then repeat the process for all the specified dependencies. If Bower cannot resolve a dependency properly, then it will prompt you for a decision and move on from there.

Library maintainers are able to tag a version in a Git repository for Bower to use as the install version, but in practice, good version tags don't always exist. The version you get may be based off the head of the master branch, and this can easily lead to unexpected conflicts. Bower and the "anarchaic" development environment of the Web don't protect developers enough to let them ignore all the nitty gritty details of our frontend dependencies. As it is, it's useful primarily as an automated installer for libraries and their dependencies, which then still get checked into a source code repository.

To install Polymer and its related dependencies, simply run the following command:

```
$ bower install polymer
```

The install command is useful to install libraries for one explicit use but by default, it doesn't keep track of any of your installed dependencies, which will make further updates, reinstallations, and tree shaking more difficult. To get this we'll need a *bower.json* configuration file, which will hold the metadata necessary to track our dependencies. We can do this nearly the same way we set up a default *package.json* with npm in Node.js:

```
$ bower init
```

After you've answered the prompts with data relevant to the project, you can save your dependencies via:

```
$ bower install --save polymer
```

This will install and save the dependencies necessary to install Polymer. Right now that will also include Polymer's *platform.js*, though in the future that will hopefully be minimized or even removed. That's part of the benefit of using something like Bower to manage dependencies: if the dependencies of your dependencies change, your installation process will manage itself accordingly.

Earlier, I mentioned that Bower and common practice dictate that all dependencies be flat and referenced via relative paths. You might have wondered how that works for local development and referencing dependencies in a maintainable way. I wish I had a great answer for you, but there are actually two (maybe three) only somewhat suitable camps on this topic right now:

1. Have your component be in the root of your development directory, with your dependencies installed as siblings in your parent directory.

   This has the side effect of polluting that parent directory with dependencies from any number of components actively in development and each of their respective dependencies.

   Development with dependencies would then look like this:

   ```
   |-- my-element
   |    |-- my-element.html
   +-- polymer
   |    |-- polymer.html
   +-- platform
        |-- platform.js
   ```

2. Have your component be two directories down in your development directory, with your dependencies installed one directory down:

   ```
   my-element
   |-- components
        |-- src
             |-- my-element.html
   ```

   This has the drawback of requiring some kind of build step in order to place the distributable element at the root so that it can reference dependencies in the consuming application's directory tree.

   With dependency installation being in the *components* directory and the "built" artifact being at the root, the end structure looks like this:

   ```
   my-element
   |-- components
   |    |-- src
   |    |    |-- my-element.html
   |    +-- polymer
   |    |    |-- polymer.html
   |    +-- platform
   ```

```
|          |-- platform.js
+-- my-element.html
```

The answer to the quick knee-jerk reaction "But how do I ignore those dependencies in source control?" is (for Git) to put the following in your *.gitignore* file:

```
components/*/
!components/src/
```

3. Don't worry about dependencies at all, and expect the host page to manage them for you.

This is the same as classic dependency management for distributed libraries right now. Libraries are created and their dependencies listed somewhere for the consuming developers to download and manage in their web pages. This has worked for nearly two decades and can work now, but it increases the user's overhead. It's also 2015, we're not cavemen, so we're going to stick with option 2. The first is too invasive and fragile, and the third is not interesting enough to put in a book.

Getting Started

To begin, set up the source root as *x-dialog* and set up the source tree so that it looks like this:

```
x-dialog
|-- index.html
|-- components
|     |-- src
|     |     |-- x-dialog.html
```

Are you on an OS X or Linux machine and find yourself making a directory that you immediately cd into frequently? Set this up in your *.bashrc* to make doing that a breeze:

```
md ()
{
    mkdir -p "$@" && cd "$@"
}
```

Now you can compress that task into the following command:

```
$ md x-dialog/components/src
$ touch x-dialog.html
```

Now I initialize the bower metadata as described earlier, by executing bower init and filling out the appropriate answers:

```
$ bower init
[?] name: x-dialog
[?] version: 0.0.0
[?] description: a dialog box web component
[?] main file: ./x-dialog.html
[?] what types of modules does this package expose? globals
[?] keywords: dialog
[?] authors: Your Name <email@email.com>
[?] license: MIT
[?] homepage: http://github.com/YOURUSER/x-dialog.html
[?] set currently installed components as dependencies? Yes
[?] add commonly ignored files to ignore list? Yes
[?] would you like to mark this package as private which prevents it from being
    accidentally published to the registry? No

{
    name: 'x-dialog',
    version: '0.0.0',
    authors: [
        Your Name <email@email.com>
    ],
    description: 'a dialog box web component',
    main: './x-dialog.html',
    moduleType: [
        'globals'
    ],
    keywords: [
        'dialog'
    ],
    license: 'MIT',
    homepage: 'http://github.com/YOURUSER/x-dialog.html',
    ignore: [
        '**/.*',
        'node_modules',
        'bower_components',
        'vendor',
        'test',
        'tests'
    ]
}

[?] Looks good? Yes
```

We'll also want to add a *.bowerrc* file so that we can specify that we want our test dependencies installed into our *components* directory:

```
{
    "directory" : "components"
}
```

If we're using Git, then we can set up our *.gitignore* file as follows:

```
components/*/
!components/src/
```

Now we can install our dependencies into our *components* directory and have them saved for the future. We'll obviously need Polymer, and since we're doing a basic port, we'll include jQuery as well. Jenga is a dependency also available in Bower, so we can install them all in one fell swoop:

```
$ bower install --save polymer jquery jenga

[ ... cut some information logging ... ]

polymer#0.3.3 components/polymer
└── platform#0.3.4

platform#0.3.4 components/platform

jenga#912f71e4cc components/jenga

jquery#2.1.1 components/jquery
```

Now we have four libraries available with one command, all installed in our *compo-nents* directory. If you `ls` inside that directory you'll see how the dependencies will look in somebody else's project (aside from the *src* directory being called *x-dialog*), so this is a great way to develop and test code.

Before we jump into coding our component, let's get our test page up and running so we can stub out our expected component API and see our work. We'll start our *index.html* file with the basic few tags that compose nearly every modern HTML file:

```
<!DOCTYPE html>
<html>
<head>
  <meta charset="UTF-8">
  <title>&lt;x-dialog&gt;</title>
</head>
<body>

</body>
</html>
```

Next we'll add some simple references to *platform.js* and import our element. It's good practice to include *platform.js* in our demo page even if our browser is set up for all native web components because it eases the process for anyone else getting into development with our element:

```
<head>
  <meta charset="UTF-8">
  <title>&lt;x-dialog&gt;</title>

  <script src="components/platform/platform.js"></script>
```

```
    <link rel="import" href="src/x-dialog.html">
  </head>
```

Now we can add our element, with some reasonable options that provide the functionality we're looking to test (actual unit testing is an entirely different matter, as we'll see in the next chapter; this is for spot checking during the porting process):

```
<body>
    <x-dialog draggable resizable></x-dialog>
</body>
```

That's it! Your final *index.html* should look like this:

```
<!DOCTYPE html>
<html>
<head>
  <meta charset="UTF-8">
  <title>&lt;x-dialog&gt;</title>

  <script src="components/platform/platform.js"></script>

  <link rel="import" href="components/src/x-dialog.html">
</head>
<body>

<x-dialog draggable resizable></x-dialog>

</body>
</html>
```

Now for the main course! There are a few Polymer boilerplate seed repositories out there, each with a slightly different style; you should look around to see what suits your fancy. For this book we'll be using the boilerplate (*https://github.com/webcompo nents/element-boilerplate*) from Addy Osmani and other contributors, slightly modified to fit our data and dependency location:

```
<!-- Import Polymer -->
<link rel="import" href="../polymer/polymer.html">

<!-- Define your custom element -->
<polymer-element name="x-dialog">

    <script>
        Polymer('x-dialog', {
            // Fires when an instance of the element is created
            created: function () {},

            // Fires when the element's initial set of children and siblings
            // are guaranteed to exist
            domReady: function () {},

            // Fires when the "<polymer-element>" has been fully prepared
            ready: function () {},
```

```
        // Fires when the element was inserted into the document
        attached: function () {},

        // Fires when the element was removed from the document
        detached: function () {},

        // Fires when an attribute was added, removed, or updated
        attributeChanged: function (attr, oldVal, newVal) {}
    });
  </script>

</polymer-element>
```

The boilerplate already includes an import for Polymer. Now we need to include our other dependency libraries, the same way we would in any other HTML file:

```
<!-- Import Polymer -->
<link rel="import" href="../polymer/polymer.html">

<script src="../jquery/dist/jquery.js"></script>
<script src="../jenga/jenga.js"></script>
```

Notice how we're including these in the root of the imported HTML document, not within the template. There are reasons to do one or the other (deferred loading, managing dependencies more granularly, etc.), but the easiest way to depend on other resources is to do it at the import level, not the custom element level.

How should we include the other sources in this book? They're written to be reusable but aren't yet Bower resources. Should they be? Maybe, but it's a good practice to wait until something proves to be reusable multiple times before abstracting it into a publishable package. In this case, we'll directly include all of the libraries we've created as source files within this component. Since we're also directly porting the existing logic into what essentially amounts to just a web component container, we can also bring along our existing implementation unchanged and see how we can use it within Polymer.

After copying those libraries to our *src* directory, our development structure now looks like this:

```
├── .bowerrc
├── bower.json
├── components
│   ├── jenga
│   ├── jquery
│   ├── platform
│   ├── polymer
│   └── src
│       ├── ApacheChief.js
│       ├── BaseComponent.js
│       ├── DialogComponent.css
```

```
|          ├── DialogComponent.js
|          ├── Duvet.js
|          ├── Shamen.js
|          └── x-dialog.html
└── index.html
```

And the preface of our component's *import.html* looks like this:

```
<!-- Import Polymer -->
<link rel="import" href="../polymer/polymer.html">

<script src="../jquery/dist/jquery.js"></script>
<script src="../jenga/jenga.js"></script>

<script src="Duvet.js"></script>
<script src="Shamen.js"></script>
<script src="ApacheChief.js"></script>
<script src="BaseComponent.js"></script>
<script src="DialogComponent.js"></script>
```

This gives us the foundation from which we started implementing the API in our original usage, selecting elements and manually "upgrading" them to dialog status. When doing a port of this level, what we're basically doing is abstracting the manual instantiation of such libraries behind an HTML API. If we think about it this way, we can start by proxying the touchpoints of our API at the point where our elements are created and in the host DOM. We'll also need a base DOM in our template so that we can render something useful:

```
<template>
    <div id="dialog" role="dialog"
        aria-labelledby="title" aria-describedby="content">
        <h2 id="title">I am a title</h2>

        <p id="content">Look at me! I am content.</p>
    </div>
</template>
```

If you checked this element out right now you'd see a pretty unexcitingly styled bit of text on the page. True, we haven't done anything useful yet, but during the porting process, any time a page isn't in an entirely broken state then we're in a good spot! Pushing forward, we know we need to style the dialog so that it is invisible by default. If we wire in our existing CSS file, we'll find our unexciting bit of text completely invisible. Success! This porting process is easy! Now we have absolutely nothing styled on the page. We need to get something showing again, so let's wire up our existing implementation and see if we can get it to display and style itself dynamically:

```
this.dialog = new Dialog({
    $el: this.$.dialog,
    draggable: this.attributes.hasOwnProperty('draggable'),
    resizable: this.attributes.hasOwnProperty('resizable'),
```

```
    alignToEl: window,
    align: 'M',
    hostQrySelector: this.$
});
this.dialog.show();
```

You'll notice a few potentially nonobvious references there. First, our $el is pointing to Polymer's ID tree hanging off the element on a $ property. This allows us to specify the element with the ID dialog in our template easily as this.$.dialog. This is also what we're using for the hostQrySelector property, specifying our root as the root to query.

Second, we're referring to the existence of our attributes draggable and resizable in order to set the Boolean values in the constructor.

Normally we wouldn't show our dialog immediately upon attaching to the DOM, but we're just trying to get to a midway point where we get our visual component up and beautiful.

Figure 15-1 shows what we see when we reload the page now.

Figure 15-1. The styled dialog

Holy moly, it worked!

Well, that's that. Book's over. Port all your jQuery widgets in an hour, right? Well, you know what? That's not too far off. If you've written well-encapsulated code, then that's close to some version of reality. Our component isn't quite done—we'll take care of the finishing touches now—but the important point is that *it works*, and it didn't take much effort.

First off, we'll want to move that show call to a method on its own so that it can be accessed off the DOM element in a consumer page. Add the following as another method on the Polymer prototype, and we're all set:

```
show: function () {
    this.dialog.show();
}
```

Now to show the dialog, we can simply add the following to our index:

```
var dialog = document.querySelector('x-dialog');
dialog.show();
```

Well, that's almost all—we'll need to listen for the `polymer-ready` event in order to catch our elements when they've been "upgraded" by Polymer:

```
window.addEventListener('polymer-ready', function () {
    var dialog = document.querySelector('x-dialog');
    dialog.show();
})
```

This will do it, and can be added anywhere in the index—before the closing </body> works perfectly.

There's one major problem with this, though. Our DOM is unchangeable, and it certainly wouldn't make sense to make a new custom element for every dialog we might have in an application. That's not a very good use for custom elements. What would a good API be defining the inner content of a dialog?

```
<x-dialog draggable resizable>
  <x-title>This is my title!</x-title>
  <x-content>This is the content of my dialog</x-content>
</x-dialog>
```

Yikes—that's possible, but it wouldn't make sense strictly for our element. This is one of the first traps people commonly fall into when dealing with custom components (especially when using Polymer, because it's just so easy). *Only make new elements for things that make sense as elements.* Maybe title and content elements do make sense, but not specifically for our use case. Let's try again:

```
<x-dialog draggable resizable>
  <header>
    <h1>This is my title!</h1>
  </header>
  <p>
    This is my content
  </p>
</x-dialog>
```

This reuses sane HTML and is much less obscure, but it also complicates the inner structure. It is viable, but what about this?

```
<x-dialog draggable resizable title="This is my title!">
  This is my content
</x-dialog>
```

This is pretty lightweight and easy to understand. It comes at the cost of limited composability of the title bar, but that might not be a bad thing. To use it effectively in our template we use a mixture of {{}} binding and the <content> tag to selectively decide where to render the "light-DOM" within our component:

```
<template>
    <link rel="stylesheet" href="DialogComponent.css">
    <div id="dialog" role="dialog">
        <h2 id="title">{{title}}</h2>

        <p id="content"><content></content></p>
    </div>
</template>
```

Here is what our final component looks like, trivially ported from a pure jQuery mindset into the world of web components:

```
<!-- Import Polymer -->
<link rel="import" href="../polymer/polymer.html">

<script src="../jquery/dist/jquery.js"></script>
<script src="../jenga/dist/jenga.js"></script>

<script src="Duvet.js"></script>
<script src="Shamen.js"></script>
<script src="ApacheChief.js"></script>
<script src="BaseComponent.js"></script>
<script src="DialogComponent.js"></script>

<!-- Define your custom element -->
<polymer-element name="x-dialog" attributes="title draggable resizable">
    <template>
        <link rel="stylesheet" href="DialogComponent.css">
        <div id="dialog" role="dialog">
            <h2 id="title">{{title}}</h2>

            <p id="content"><content></content></p>
        </div>
    </template>
    <script>
        Polymer('x-dialog', {
            attached: function() {
                this.dialog = new Dialog({
                    $el: this.$.dialog,
                    draggable: this.attributes.hasOwnProperty('draggable'),
                    resizable: this.attributes.hasOwnProperty('resizable'),
                    alignToEl: window,
                    align: 'M',
                    hostQrySelector: this.$
                });
            },
            show: function() {
```

```
        this.dialog.show();
      }
    });
  </script>

</polymer-element>
```

That Was Easy—A Little Too Easy!

This simple process goes to show how easy it can be to embrace web components. Though, having said that, all we really did was go from a jQuery implementation of a dialog box to a jQuery implementation of a dialog box wrapped with Polymer.

There's nothing wrong with jQuery, but I can understand some of you might have felt a little robbed there. The beautiful world of web components promises progress, large steps forward, and a hearty "goodbye" to the legacy of today. jQuery has traditionally been used to iron out the wrinkles of inconsistent, ancient browsers. Does jQuery have a place in the world of Polymer?

jQuery in a Polymer World

Any professional that relies on his or her toolbox—whether a woodworker, mecha-nin, or software developer—is likely to recall a time when a new tool was released that promised the world and purported to make the tools of the past irrelevant, clearing up valuable space in the workshop.

Polymer and jQuery are indeed tools, not frameworks. They don't define how an application should be developed; in fact, they don't even provide you with the tools necessary to make a maintainable application. Multiple tools aren't a problem, but can be a "code smell" for browser-based applications. One of the biggest issues in browser JavaScript, with its poor (absent) dependency management and module system, is that popular tools end up having a lot of overlap in order to reduce their own dependencies on others. Including multiple tools that overlap bloats your code base and increases the distributable size.

Polymer, being more modern and able to define its path based on current best practices, tries to be more focused (though it still includes the kitchen sink when it comes to polyfills). On the other hand, jQuery includes an incredible array of features that can make it seem oversized, and the library itself is not uncommonly seen as a red flag, indicating inefficient or amateur development practices. This is a wild oversimplification, but nonetheless it has inspired attempts at creating lighterweight implementations, like Xepto.js and Minified.js.

It's important to know what a library is offering you when you include it. Every library brings in a potentially substantial download and parse cost, and responsible developers should make sure all that code brings more value than it costs.

What Does jQuery Provide?

Do you *know* and *use* everything that jQuery provides? You should make sure. It may well all be excellent and useful, but how much of it you actually use is definitely worth thinking about.

At the least, jQuery provides:

- An intuitive chaining API
- Utility functions for objects, arrays, and strings
- DOM selection
- DOM traversal
- DOM manipulation
- CSS animations
- Normalized CSS getters/setters
- Promise/deferred implementation
- AJAX methods
- An event API

This is not meant to be an exhaustive list; these are just some of the most commonly used features of jQuery. It's hard to get a good overview of what jQuery features a project uses, but once you go through the practice once, it gives you a great baseline of what types of things are common in different scenarios.

How much jQuery do you think we've used in the book so far? Let's find out! The quickest way to determine the value of something is to go without it, so let's go ahead and rip jQuery out of the dependencies and reload the page. It'll all work, right? Of course not. We're about to embark on a horrible exercise that everyone attempts at least once in their browser development lives.

We're going to remove jQuery.

Removing jQuery

Of course, the first errors we get are just `undefined` errors because we're trying to pass jQuery into the immediately invoked function expression (IIFE) that contains all our library code. After taking care of that, we can start stepping through the jQuery method invocations and try to port each individual one to a generic method. Remember, if we're working with web components and Polymer, we're already stating that we're working with a very modern matrix of supported browsers. There are a lot of common APIs that replace jQuery methods.

We're not going to go through all the replacements necessary, but we are going to go through the general themes and how the replacements might work.

The immediate case we run into is using jQuery to create DOM elements, style them with an object filled with CSS properties, and append one onto another:

```
//Duvet.js
var $inner = $('<div>test</div>').css(innerCss);
var $outer = $('<div></div>').css(outerCss).append($inner);
```

One thing that becomes immediately apparent is just how much code jQuery saves us from writing. That is actually a nutty amount of functionality in a miniscule number of characters.

We're not going to work hard at implementing the best solutions for these problems right now. The goal is simply to remove jQuery, so the biggest benefit is abstracting out any changes for refactoring later. No effort is made here for cross-compatibility, edge cases, or security:

```
function htmlify(html) {
    var div = document.createElement('div');
    div.innerHTML = html;
    return div.children[0];
}
```

The CSS method looks like it's doing a lot of work up front, but at the end of the day, a large amount of what it's doing is merging an object with the style property of an HTML element. We can do that easily by creating our own extend-like function:

```
function mergeObjects(dest /* varargs */) {
    var args = Array.prototype.slice.call(arguments, 1);
    args.forEach(function(obj) {
        for (var i in obj) {
            if (obj.hasOwnProperty(i)) {
                dest[i] = obj[i]
            }
        }
    });
    return dest;
}
```

The preceding jQuery code then becomes:

```
var $inner = htmlify('<div>test</div>');
mergeObjects($inner.style, innerCss);

var $outer = htmlify('<div></div>');
mergeObjects($outer.style, outerCss);
```

```
$outer.appendChild($inner);
```

Not quite as terse, but entirely approachable. The bulk of the cleanups immediately thereafter amount to changing:

- `append()` to `appendChild()`
- References from the first collection element to the variable itself (`$element[0]` to `element`)
- `extend()` to `mergeObject()`
- `clone()` to `cloneNode(true)`
- `el.find()` to `el.querySelector()` or `el.querySelectorAll()`
- `el.css(obj)` to `mergeObjects(el.style, obj)`
- `el.parent()` to `el.parentElement()`

The first major hiccup comes in the event binding for ApacheChief.js and Shamen.js. These use event namespaces, which is an entirely separate concept added by jQuery that allows you to group events by application or widget for easy unbinding or querying later. Without this, you'll need to more carefully manage your bindings in order to prevent memory leaks and odd behavior. It's certainly doable, but it's a really nice feature. Event handling in JavaScript is a very sensitive proposition prone to human error, and a management framework provides a lot of benefit—not so much because events are necessarily hard to create or unbind, but because a framework provides an interface that proxies all that interaction so the event handlers can be referenced and dereferenced automatically later.

Pushing through for the sake of the exercise, we come across a few more simple things to change:

- `width()` to `innerWidth()`
- Ensuring that assignments to CSS position integers end with px

The last serious issue that we come across is getting the positions of elements. JQuery's method `el.getPosition` does more work than we can easily replace, so we can modify the original jQuery source to provide us with a workable shim:

```
function getPosition(elem) {
    var offsetParent, offset,
        parentOffset = { top: 0, left: 0 };

    offset = elem.getBoundingClientRect();

    // Fixed elements are offset from window (parentOffset = {top:0, left: 0},
    // because it is its only offset parent
```

```
if ( elem.style.position !== "fixed" ) {
    // Get *real* offsetParent
    offsetParent = elem.offsetParent;

    // Get correct offsets
    offset = {
        top: offset.top + window.pageYOffset -
            document.documentElement.clientTop,
        left: offset.left + window.pageXOffset -
            document.documentElement.clientLeft
    };

    // Add offsetParent borders
    parentOffset.top += offsetParent.style.borderTopWidth = true;
    parentOffset.left += offsetParent.style.borderLeftWidth = true;
}

// Subtract parent offsets and element margins
return {
    top: offset.top - parentOffset.top - elem.style.marginTop,
    left: offset.left - parentOffset.left - elem.style.marginLeft
};
}
```

After this our element is dependency-free outside of Polymer. We are resizable, draggable, and showable!

As we've already seen, we could even remove Polymer to get a web component that relied on *no outside code*. That's kind of fun sounding isn't it? We have a brand new HTML element with 100% pure JavaScript, and it wasn't even that hard. But… have you tried to load that component in Firefox? Or Safari? Or Android? What about the memory leaks we neglected to account for in the HTML creation? What about *everything else*?

The Verdict on jQuery

JQuery gets a lot of flak because a lot of its methods mask seemingly trivial tasks that have their own native counterparts. What people often forget is that jQuery excels at leveling the playing field, ironing out cross-browser issues, providing consistent APIs for inconsistent browser methods, and providing excellent wrappers for difficult or frustrating aspects of the DOM.

You can absolutely work without jQuery, but the simple fact is that you'll probably want *something* in its place to provide you with the utility, consistency, and compatibility jQuery offers. If you resign yourself to needing something, then you can choose an existing alternative or attempt to create and maintain one yourself. At first glance, an internally maintained implementation sounds perfectly reasonable, but as you round each corner and find a new mountain of browser bugs to accommodate, the task quickly becomes a frustrating beast. In early 2014 Rick Waldron put together a quick roundup (*http://bit.ly/dwc-waldron*) of all the cross-browser bugs that jQuery accounts for, and it is anything but light reading. Certainly, a lot of these issues are for browsers that wouldn't be in a support matrix for a website implementing web components, but there are some that would. Regardless, it is a certainty that jQuery will continue to fix bugs found in future browsers, so you can imagine the list shrinking in some areas of legacy support but growing to account for new bugs.

There is a place for jQuery, both now and in the future. If your code base makes substantial use of jQuery, don't worry about it. If you want to write a web component and find the need for utilities that jQuery will provide, you're not hurting much by depending on it.

Summary

In this chapter we learned how to incorporate current philosophies behind widget creation into the wild world of Polymerized web components. We also learned that a lot of our existing ideas are still relevant and that Polymerized web components are an excellent technology to work into existing code in a piecemeal fashion. Polymer provides intuitive hooks inward and a valuable interface outward that can benefit any encapsulated widget that you've written in the past.

We also learned that jQuery, while often jeered at for being a relic of the past, still includes valuable logic in a familiar package. Polymer doesn't replace jQuery, and even if you have a tremendous amount of code wrapped up in jQuery plugins, you can still benefit from Polymer and web components.

CHAPTER 16

Testing Web Components

Jarrod Overson

The biggest problem with any new technology is fitting it into an existing flow with minimal turbulence. The pieces of the flow that are subject to the most friction are:

Development (IDE assistance, documentation)
> Where do you go for questions? How will you be able to solve problems that come up?

Maintenance
> How stable is the technology? Is it undergoing massive changes? Will going back to code written with this tech one year from now be simple or a nightmare?

Testing
> How are unit tests written? How testable is code written with this new technology?

Building
> Does this new technology affect the build process at all?

Deploying
> Do your deployments change? What metrics need to be tracked in order to measure the impact of the new technology?

It's important to run through at least these checkpoints in order to get a high-level overview of the problems you might face, although it might be tempting to charge forward once you've gotten past the first hurdle because that's usually the primary focus of technology marketing.

The biggest problem with web components, in my humble opinion, is the lack of testability and the complications that web components introduce when testing, especially at this phase. It might seem silly; at the end of the day we're just talking about HTML elements, which have been around since the middle ages (approximately). That may be true, but with the substantial polyfills that are used in different combinations for every browser on the market right now, the need for automated cross-browser testing is critical, and the tools that normally help us with that task aren't yet perfectly suited for web component testing.

There are a number of different ways to test browser-destined code, each of which has its drawbacks when testing web components (in their current state) and web component polyfills. Here we'll look at a few of the popular testing tools for web applications and see how they stack up.

PhantomJS 1

PhantomJS (*http://phantomjs.org/*), as of version 1.9, is 100% out of the equation when testing web components due to its lack of support for the core technologies and the inability to work with some of the polyfills the Polymer group provides. The author, Ariya Hidayat, is at work on version 2.0, but as of yet it's unknown how well

PhantomJS will support web components in the future. This immediately kills a lot of common tasks and tools that leverage PhantomJS for headless testing and will likely affect a lot of people's testing in Continuous Integration (CI) environments.

PhantomJS 2

By the time you read this book, PhantomJS 2 will have been released. It provides a capable headless browser with which to test shimmed web components. QTWebKit, upon which PhantomJS is based, does not have native support for web component technologies, but the shims go a long way toward providing a headless solution to unit testing web components. Polymer functions and behaves well in the environment and web components are of interested to the PhantomJS team, so the current level of support can be expected to be maintained or improved.

Selenium WebDriver

Selenium WebDriver (*http://bit.ly/dwc-webdriver*) is, by and large, the most commonly used tool for automating web page UI testing, and it is almost completely broken as soon as you include *platform.js* on your page (as of version 0.2.4). This is noted and the Google team is aware of it, but it means that if you maintain a large suite of automated frontend tests, they may *all* be rendered useless by the simple introduction of a single Polymer component—*regardless of whether that component is even being tested*.

These are horror stories that, if told around a campfire in the woods, would send some developers running for their sleeping bags, praying for morning to come and the nightmares to stop.

It's not all fright and fear, though, and given the progress everyone is making, some of these issues may be rectified shortly after this book is published. Don't take anything in this book as gospel (until the second or third revision, at least). These topics are discussed because they hold true at the moment and are important to be aware of.

Karma

Fortunately, one of the best modern day choices in testing browser code, Karma (*http://bit.ly/dwc-karma*) (formerly Testacular), is still a top-of-the-line choice for unit testing Polymer components. There are some quirks and a few edge cases that aren't well supported, but it's still a solid option that will probably expand to fill the role better in the future.

If you're already familiar with Karma, you'll probably still want to have a separate configuration in order to manage maintainability of the test framework going forward. It is highly likely that the practices outlined here will evolve and the plugins will change, so you don't want the Polymer testing to get in the way of established and stable testing elsewhere.

For those just getting started with Karma, it's a Node.js tool that can be installed globally with its per-project plugins installed locally as developer dependencies. You can install Karma via npm as follows:

```
$ npm install -g karma-cli
```

This will give you the tool that then delegates to a local installation of the Karma libraries. The base library you'll need for Karma is, appropriately, `karma`:

```
$ npm install karma
```

Karma requires a sometimes *extensive* configuration, but thankfully, the boilerplate and some sensible defaults can be automatically generated via the `init` command from the Karma CLI. This can only be done after installing a local version of Karma, so don't skip the previous step before running this command:

```
$ karma init
```

This will guide you through a series of questions that will help you to get started with most common testing implementations. We're going to be working with Mocha and Chai, and you can choose the browsers you want to run when you get to the prompts. It's recommended that you run at least one other browser outside of Chrome in order to ensure that you are using as many of the polyfills as possible. Chrome has full support for web components from version 36 onward, so the behavior and performance could be substantially different.

Outside of what is automated with `init`, a good set of modules to start with is:

`karma`
> 5H3 base Karma library

`karma-mocha`
> A plugin that wires Mocha into Karma

`karma-chai`
> A plugin for the Chai assertion library

`karma-chrome-launcher`
> A launcher for Chrome

`karma-firefox-launcher`
> A launcher for Firefox

`karma-webcomponent-helpers`
> Some helper scripts to assist with loading fixtures for web component testing

These can be installed in one fell swoop via npm:

```
$ npm install --save-dev karma karma-mocha karma-chai \
karma-chrome-launcher karma-firefox-launcher \
karma-webcomponent-helpers
```

Part of the complication of using Polymer as our web component framework is that we are writing and storing all of our base component files as HTML and importing them as relative HTML imports. This is 100% foreign to almost every existing use case, and *no* testing framework supports this at all yet. Some may support loading fixtures, which can be used depending on the implementation, but this is largely a problem that still needs to be solved.

A unit testing framework specific to Polymer is something that could have potential, as could a unit testing framework for whatever web component manager ends up leading the pack in the next 12 months. There are not yet any true best practices for testing web components or Polymer, so take our recommendations with a grain of salt. They have worked, and currently do work, but as and when something new comes along, it should be evaluated with preference.

The primary tasks that need to be addressed immediately are:

1. Find a way to dynamically load HTML imports from the test specs.
2. Create HTML snippets that Polymer can recognize and upgrade before the tests run.

To this end, we've isolated some practices that have worked in the past into the Karma plugin `karma-webcomponent-helpers`. It's a minimal set of assistant helpers that will probably grow as necessary.

Making Karma aware of what files to automatically load and serve is also accomplished a little differently than normal. Since we're not loading script files as our source, we can't use Karma's default configuration. Our files config ends up looking like this:

```
// list of files/patterns to load in the browser
files: [
  'components/platform/platform.js',
  {
  pattern:'components/src/**/*',
  included: false,
  watched: true,
  served: true
  },
  {
  pattern:'components/**/*.html',
  included: false,
  watched: false,
  served: true
  },
  {
```

```
   pattern:'components/**/*.css',
   included: false,
   watched: false,
   served: true
  },
  {
   pattern:'components/**/*.js',
   included: false,
   watched: false,
   served: true
  },
  'test/**/*.spec.js'
 ],
```

The first and most obvious thing to note are the first and last lines: we're loading *platform.js* first in order to ensure polyfills are loaded, and the last line includes all the test scripts that actually define our test JavaScript, with assertions and all.

The middle four lines define a wide net of *stuff* that Karma should be aware of but shouldn't actually include in our template HTML (`included: false`). The first line is a pattern that matches everything in our *components/src/* directory and lets Karma know it should watch those files for changes (`watched: true`). All of the patterns also specify `served: true`, meaning that, if we ask for a resource, Karma should serve it on its own HTTP server. This allows us to import HTML and have the browser ask for whatever is referenced without us explicitly defining it here.

For those familiar with unit testing browser code, this probably looked ugly until you got to that last line. This method of dependency management means that we can just import our HTML file, and it will include everything it needs to in order to run properly. Without this, we'd need to make sure we manually included and determined the order of third-party libraries like Jenga and jQuery along with our internal source. This can easily lead to lists dozens of lines long with sensitive ordering dependencies that need to be managed in parallel with the code and other test pages themselves.

Our entire *karma.conf.js* follows. The only other major changes to the default Karma configuration are to the `plugins`, `browsers`, and `frameworks` properties:

```
module.exports = function(config) {
  config.set({

    // base path that will be used to resolve all patterns (e.g. files, exclude)
    basePath: '',


    // frameworks to use
    // available frameworks: https://npmjs.org/browse/keyword/karma-adapter
    frameworks: ['mocha', 'chai', 'webcomponent-helpers'],

    polymerTest: {
    },
```

```
// list of files/patterns to load in the browser
files: [
  'components/platform/platform.js',
  'test/**/*.spec.js',
  {
   pattern:'components/src/**/*',
   included: false,
   watched: true,
   served: true
  },
  {
   pattern:'components/**/*.html',
   included: false,
   watched: false,
   served: true
  },
  {
   pattern:'components/**/*.css',
   included: false,
   watched: false,
   served: true
  },
  {
   pattern:'components/**/*.js',
   included: false,
   watched: false,
   served: true
  }
],


// list of files to exclude
exclude: [
],


// preprocess matching files before serving them to the browser
// available preprocessors:
// https://npmjs.org/browse/keyword/karma-preprocessor
preprocessors: {
},


// test results reporter to use
// possible values: 'dots', 'progress'
// available reporters: https://npmjs.org/browse/keyword/karma-reporter
reporters: ['progress'],


// web server port
```

```
    port: 9876,


    // enable / disable colors in the output (reporters and logs)
    colors: true,


    // level of logging
    // possible values:
    // config.LOG_DISABLE
    // config.LOG_ERROR
    // config.LOG_WARN
    // config.LOG_INFO
    // config.LOG_DEBUG
    logLevel: config.LOG_INFO,


    // enable/disable watching file and executing tests when any file changes
    autoWatch: true,


    // start these browsers
    // available browser launchers:
    // https://npmjs.org/browse/keyword/karma-launcher
    browsers: ['Chrome', 'Firefox'],

    plugins: [
      'karma-webcomponent-helpers',
      'karma-mocha',
      'karma-chai',
      'karma-chrome-launcher',
      'karma-firefox-launcher'
    ],

    // Continuous Integration mode
    // if true, Karma captures browsers, runs the tests, and exits
    singleRun: false
  });
};
```

Test Specs

Our tests largely follow standard Mocha design with some boilerplate setup and tear-down. If you're unfamiliar with Mocha, it is designed to follow behavior-driven development (BDD) practices and has functions named as such. Mocha itself is a fairly lightweight harness for the organization of blocks that include assertions. Every spec starts off as a description of what feature is being tested:

```
describe('<x-dialog>', function () {



});
```

The `karma-webcomponent-helpers` plugin provides us with some useful functions to
both import an HTML document (as a proper HTML import) and create elements.
Nothing fancy, but both things we'll want to do regularly when testing web components. At the start of our tests we'll need to import our custom component. That
can be done with Mocha's `before` method, which runs once at the start of its
`describe` block:

```
describe('<x-dialog>', function () {

  before(function(done){
    helpers.importHref('./base/components/src/x-dialog.html', function () {
      Polymer.whenPolymerReady(done);
    });
  });

});
```

The `helpers.injectElement(url, callback)` function takes a callback that is called
when the `load` event is dispatched on the related `<link>` element. Since we want to
wait for our import to load before running our tests, we make this an asynchronous
task simply by specifying a function argument as part of what is passed to `before`.
Mocha will assume any of its methods that take in an argument are asynchronous and
will wait for that argument to be called before moving on. This is important to note
because it is not uncommon during refactoring to eliminate the need for some asynchronous call, thus deleting the subsequent call to `done`, which then hangs your tests
without much description of why. We also ensure we are avoiding all the race condi-
tions we can by delegating our asynchronous completion function to Polymer's when
`PolymerReady` method. This is a handy method that is analogous to the globally
dispatched `polymer-ready` event, with the added sugar of immediately calling the
passed handler if `polymer-ready` has already been dispatched.

In order to create an element that we can test appropriately we can use another helper
method, `helpers.injectElement(snippet, callback)`, which will inject the passed
HTML into the body of the document, return the created element, and run the callback after execution has been yielded to the browser for processing.

The creation of the element should be done before actual tests are executed and the
element should be destroyed after every test in order to ensure the state is consistent
and uncontaminated for each test scenario:

```
describe('<x-dialog>', function () {
  var element;
```

```
before(function(done){
  helpers.importHref(
      './base/components/src/x-dialog.html', function () {
    Polymer.whenPolymerReady(done);
  });
});

beforeEach(function(done){
  element = helpers.injectElement(
      '<x-dialog title="Hello World">Content</x-dialog>', done);
});

afterEach(function () {
  element.remove();
})

});
```

Now the structure is well set up for a decent romp through unit testing. Tests are written as part of it blocks, which encourages the test author to describe the tests from the perspective of interaction, not the perspective of the developer. This sounds trivial, but it's a valuable perspective shift that allows you to focus on what's important, not what actually exists. Consider this example test plan:

1. Test the ignition.
2. Test the engine.
3. Test the tire capacity and durability.

versus this one:

1. It should turn on when you pull the pull cord.
2. It should spin the blade when the engine is on.
3. It should be able to withstand bumping into rocks and walls.

This is an obviously contrived example, but the second method of explaining what is being tested better outlines what is important in the tests so that it can be focused on. Getting back to our example, we can specify the following tests:

```
it('should instantiate via a constructor', function () {
  var dialog = new XDialog();
  expect(dialog).to.be.an.instanceof(HTMLElement)
});

it('should have a title', function () {
  expect(element).to.be.an.instanceof(HTMLElement)
  assert.equal(element.title, 'Hello World');
});
```

```
it('should open without throwing an error', function () {
  element.show();
});
```

Notice how we're testing the most minimal set of functionality per test. This ensures that failures are obvious in our scope and also reduces the effort necessary to write tests. Sure, these tests could be made better, but they serve as an example as to what can be done here. The full test spec looks like this:

```
describe('<x-dialog>', function () {
  var element;

  before(function(done){
    helpers.importHref('./base/components/src/x-dialog.html', function () {
      Polymer.whenPolymerReady(done);
    });
  });

  beforeEach(function(done){
    element = helpers.injectElement(
        '<x-dialog title="Hello World">Content</x-dialog>', done);
  });

  it('should instantiate via a constructor', function () {
    var dialog = new XDialog();
    expect(dialog).to.be.an.instanceof(HTMLElement)
  });

  it('should have a title', function () {
    expect(element).to.be.an.instanceof(HTMLElement)
    assert.equal(element.title, 'Hello World');
  });

  it('should open', function () {
    element.show();
  });

  afterEach(function () {
    element.remove();
  })

});
```

Running Our Tests

Our tests can be run via the command line simply by executing karma start (output truncated where necessary to fit within the page margins):

```
$ karma start
INFO [karma]: Karma v0.12.19 server started at http://localhost:9876/
```

```
INFO [launcher]: Starting browser Chrome
INFO [launcher]: Starting browser Firefox
INFO [Firefox 31.0.0 (Mac OS X 10.9)]: Connected on socket fsQW with id
INFO [Chrome 36.0.1985 (Mac OS X 10.9.2)]: Connected on socket Gl7a with id …
Firefox 31.0.0 (Mac OS X 10.9) WARN: 'platform.js is not the first script …

Chrome 36.0.1985 (Mac OS X 10.9.2): Executed 3 of 3 SUCCESS (0.201 secs … secs)
Firefox 31.0.0 (Mac OS X 10.9): Executed 3 of 3 SUCCESS (0.222 secs … secs)
TOTAL: 6 SUCCESS
```

This will also watch all of our source files, rerunning tests as anything changes. If we need to debug our code within a browser, we can click the "DEBUG" button in the upper righthand corner of the Karma test page that gets loaded in each of the spawned browsers (see Figure 16-1).

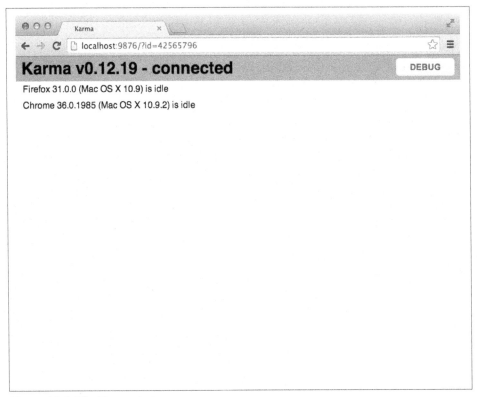

Figure 16-1. The Karma test page

This will bring you to a blank page allowing you to open the browser's developer tools and inspect at will.

Running these tests manually is useful, but unit tests aren't worth much unless they are run automatically. In the next chapter we'll be incorporating our build process and will see how Karma and other testing tools can play a role as part of a larger task chain.

Summary

A lot of exciting promises have been made about web components. In this chapter, we faced one of the hard truths—lack of testability—and provided you with a possible route through. Solid unit tests are the foundation on which maintainable applications are made, and without them, teams can find themselves floundering around trying to keep their heads above water.

Unit tests automated via JavaScript and Karma are, in our eyes, the best way to test Polymerized web components right now. Tools will absolutely emerge to fill in the gaps, but this may be your largest pain point right now.

To be honest, though, there are many people and teams who don't actually do very thorough unit testing. I know, it amazes even me, but it's true. If you happen to be part of such a team (I won't tell anybody), then I can assure you Polymer and web components *will help the maintainability of your application*. The concrete line of demarcation with web components—HTML tags, attributes, and associated public JavaScript methods—helps to encapsulate logic in a very strict manner. This strictness and the natural desire to adhere to it benefit everyone in the long run.

CHAPTER 17

Packaging and Publishing

Jarrod Overson

Build processes in JavaScript are a subject of common debate. On the one hand, there is a beautifully romantic simplicity in being able to author code that gets delivered directly to an end user and runs without modification. There are people who optimize for that simplicity, using it as a creative constraint to encourage simple and clever programming. On the other hand, authored code and delivered code exist in different environments and are read by different machines. On the client side, the user's machines parses the code and runs it to deliver the end user experience. On the development side, the machine is *you*, and you parse code in a very different way than an executable interpreter. Good development practice may actually result in very poorly optimized code when it comes to delivery and parsing.

When acknowledging those differences, an intermediary process that translates the code from one environment to the deployable artifact for the other seems like an obvious necessity and something that one should optimize for from the start.

The important aspects to consider when determining the extent of a build process are the same as for anything else: what is the cost and value of one choice versus another? It's impossible for anyone to tell you what you *should* do in your particular situation, so it's important to test it yourself.

Oftentimes one of the biggest red flags in browser code is the number of requests being made, and it is trivial to make more requests than you realize when importing a single HTML file. This is more of a concern today than it used to be because while there has never been a great way to refer to and load dependencies in widget code like this, now, one poorly optimized HTML import can easily link to dozens of other resources—and we (and our implementers) don't want to worry about things like that.

Our element includes a number of external scripts that aren't immediately reused anywhere else. It also includes dependencies on Polymer, jQuery, and Jenga, which are third-party libraries that we shouldn't be worrying about at the moment; our main concern is all the internal code. In traditional widgets and modular JavaScript code developed to be distributed, the build and delivery process often consists simply of the minification and concatenation of all the project's files into one distributable, compressed file. You see this regularly with libraries like jQuery (and even Polymer's *platform.js*): there is an uncompressed (though maybe concatenated) deployable called *jquery.js* and another smaller distributable called *jquery.min.js*. The source of jQuery is actually a couple dozen AMD modules that can be used independently but go through an extensive build process to arrive at the deployable artifact that optimizes the footprint, produces source maps, and generates multiple versions of "jQuery" proper.

For code meant to be delivered as HTML files and imported by way of HTML imports, though, we can't use all the same tools because we're potentially linking to a variety of resources that need to be embedded into the HTML file itself. UglifyJS, Esmangle, and the like only work for JavaScript. Fortunately, the Polymer team already has us covered here and has been working on a tool specifically for this problem.

Vulcanize

Vulcanize is the first major solution for packaging up web components for deployment: it provides a way to manage custom elements written with Polymer in external HTML files. It is both a library and a tool written in JavaScript on top of Node.js and can be installed via npm. Since Vulcanize is a library as well it can be incorporated into build tools, but the command-line functionality is a great way to test its viability before going through the effort of fitting it into a build.

You can install it globally in order to easily access its executable, `vulcanize`, from your command line:

```
$ npm install -g vulcanize
vulcanize@0.3.1
├── nopt@2.2.1 (abbrev@1.0.5)
├── clean-css@2.1.8 (commander@2.1.0)
├── cheerio@0.15.0 (entities@1.0.0, CSSselect@0.4.1, lodash@2.4.1, ...)
└── uglify-js@2.4.15 (uglify-to-browserify@1.0.2, async@0.2.10, ...)
```

Node.js Command-Line Tools

Vulcanize follows one of the current established best practices for command-line tools written on Node.js, the "library-first" pattern. This pattern establishes, first and foremost, that the functionality of a tool should be delivered in a reusable library while the command-line interface (CLI) exists only as a very minimal wrapper between the command line and the library, passing options largely unchanged.

Consider the `vulcanize` options:

```
$ vulcanize --help
vulcanize: Concatenate a set of Web Components into one file

Usage:
  vulcanize [OPTIONS] <html file>*

Options:
  --output, -o: Output file name (defaults to vulcanized.html)
  --verbose, -v: More verbose logging
  --help, -h, -?: Print this message
  --config: Read the given config file
  --strip, -s: Remove comments and empty text nodes
  --csp: Extract inline scripts to a separate file (uses <output filename>.js)
  --inline: The opposite of CSP mode, inline all assets (script and css) into
            the document
  --csp --inline: Bundle all javascript (inline and external) into <output
                  filename>.js

Config:
  JSON file for additional options

  {
    "excludes": {
      "imports": [ "regex-to-exclude" ],
      "styles": [ "regex-to-exclude" ],
      "scripts": [ "regex-to-exclude" ],
    }
  }
```

You can see where some concessions were made (by way of the JSON configuration). There isn't an attempt to fully encompass every conceivable option by way of CLI arguments; the important arguments are covered and the rest can be configured via a simple JSON object.

This allows `vulcanize` to be reused in ways that the authors didn't necessarily intend. For a tool like `vulcanize`, this might mean incorporating it as part of tasks in tools like `grunt`, `gulp`, or `broccoli`. For other command-line tools like `jshint` or `coffee script`, this could also mean allowing the library to be consumed by the browser. If all of these tools were written "CLI-first," this would be much less of a possibility.

Running `vulcanize` without any options other than the input document produces a *vulcanized.html* file next to your input:

```
$ vulcanize components/src/x-dialog.html

$ ls -l components/src/*.html
-rw-r--r-- 7224 components/src/vulcanized.html
-rw-r--r-- 1303 components/src/x-dialog.html
```

Right away we notice that 1) `vulcanize` did *something*, since our output file is larger than the input, and 2) it did it *fast*. (The curious among you will also have noticed that `vulcanize` didn't tell us a damned thing about what it *did* do—and, no, `--verbose` doesn't change that.)

By default, `vulcanize` inlines imported HTML and leaves linked JavaScript in place. Depending on your use cases, that may be exactly what you want, but we're looking to produce a fully encapsulated deliverable that can be imported easily. In this case, the `--inline` option is exactly what we want:

```
$ vulcanize --inline components/src/x-dialog.html

$ ls -l components/src/*html
-rw-r--r--  357090 components/src/vulcanized.html
-rw-r--r--    1301 components/src/x-dialog.html
```

Clearly, a 357 KB web component isn't what we're going for. We didn't specify what we wanted to inline, so `vulcanize` inlined Polymer, jQuery, and Jenga along with all of our dialog's source. That's rarely what anyone would want to do, and fortunately it's possible to configure what to include and exclude via an external JSON configuration file. I have a habit of prefixing the names of optional configuration files with a dot, so I've called this file *.vulcanize.json*. It looks like this:

```
{
    "excludes": {
        "imports": [
            "polymer"
        ],
        "scripts": [
            "jquery",
            "jenga"
        ]
    }
}
```

Here we specify that we're not looking to import the `polymer` HTML file, nor are we looking to inline `jquery` or `jenga`. Those values are all regular expressions, so they would match any files that include the terms `polymer`, `jenga`, or `jquery`. We don't have any other files, but this is worth noting in case you do have anything that might get matched (a common practice for `jQuery` plugins is to name them *jquery.<plugin>*.

js, and it's not unreasonable to think that some plugins may be better inlined than depended upon externally). With this configuration file in place, let's have another go:

```
$ vulcanize --config .vulcanize.json --inline components/src/x-dialog.html
```

```
$ ls -l components/src/*html
-rw-r--r--  30405 components/src/vulcanized.html
-rw-r--r--   1301 components/src/x-dialog.html
```

This is substantially better. But we don't want our built file to be called *vulcanized.html*, nor do we want it in our *src* folder, remember? This is where our choice of directory structure starts paying off when incorporated as part of a build process with a distributable artifact.

Artifacts, Distributables, and Builds, Oh My!

The terms used here may be foreign to some people, but they go a long way toward describing an end goal effectively. "Widgets" and similar terms aren't often appropriate because they can mean just about anything to different people. Let's take a look at a few definitions:

Build process
> A pipeline that is initiated and completes on its own.

Build
> An individual run of a build pipeline. There can be successful builds and failed builds.

Artifact
> A by-product.

Distributable
> A self-contained file (or limited set of files) that can be distributed on its own.

Consumer
> The end user (developer).

Publish
> The act of making a distributable artifact available to consumers.

So, the term "build artifact" simply means a by-product of the build: something that does not exist as part of the source code and probably shouldn't be tracked as source code.[1] Analysis reports and test results are also build artifacts, but they are not (likely) distributable artifacts.

---

1 JavaScript developers often do check their distributable artifacts into source control because of the nature of how JavaScript is used and because there is no good browser code registry. Even so, the artifacts are treated like versioned binaries, not editable source code with changes tracked by commits.

An example outside of web components and Polymer would be a library written in CoffeeScript. The CoffeeScript source code is the important stuff to be tracked by version control, and the build process produces executable JavaScript that is published as the distributable artifact.

In this case, our distributable artifact needs to enable us to be imported at the base of our directory structure, both for ease of use and, critically, to be able to access dependencies relatively in the exact same way we access them in our *src* folder. This can be done simply with the following command run in the root of our project directory:

```
$ vulcanize --config .vulcanize.json \
--inline components/src/x-dialog.html \
-o x-dialog.html
```

This does just what we want, but there is a concern we're not addressing. Some of our users may want to be able to use our component in an environment that is secured by a security model that supports the W3C's Content Security Policy (CSP) recommendation (*http://www.w3.org/TR/CSP/*). This is a security measure that prevents, among other things, inline scripts from being executed. Vulcanize supports this handily in a couple of different ways. The method that works best for us is to have Vulcanize aggregate, concatenate, and extract all scripts to a separate file:

```
$ vulcanize --config .vulcanize.json \
--inline --csp components/src/x-dialog.html \
-o x-dialog.html
```

In order to accommodate both styles, we named the output file *x-dialog-csp.html*.

The Importance of Automation

Now we have two commands we need to run upon every build, both with a number of arguments that can easily be forgotten, munged, or transposed between commands. Even with only one command like this, it is incredibly important that it be condensed down to a single idiotproof script. Why? Because builds are always the last step. They are the step we rush because the "important" stuff is done. We publish prematurely. We shout, "Let me just commit this and I'll be done." We run builds and leave without checking the results.

Builds are the shopping carts of the developer world. They are the task at the end of all the real work that isn't accounted for, is trivialized, and isn't a priority.

Build pipelines without automation force you to bring the shopping cart all the way back to the front of the store every single time. Automated builds are the equivalent of having a handy SuperMart™ employee waiting to whisk that cart away from you as soon as you are done. Think about it: do you *always* return your cart exactly where you should? No. You don't. No one does.

> And even if you *really* want to believe that *you* do it, your coworker doesn't. That contributor to your project doesn't. The user playing with your code won't.

In order to keep these commands under control, we should put them in some sort of manageable automated build process. There are an infinite number of ways this can be done, depending on your background. It's not as easy as having a *build.sh* and a *build.bat*, because that would still require two commands to be run, maintained, and kept in sync.

If you come from a Unixy upbringing, `make` is an extremely popular and battle-tested tool that seems to fit the bill entirely. The only major problem is that it isn't easy to install and use on Windows, and once the commands start scaling you run into cross-compatibility issues at every turn.

Coming from a Java background? If so, `ant` is probably your go-to and can very easily be made to automate a couple of shell commands with a few deft swishes of the XML pen. It's a bit heavy-handed, but it can definitely work.

If you come from the Ruby world, `rake` is very popular and can easily work just as well as the previous two tools. One of the benefits of `rake`, though, is how well it ties into Ruby tools and libraries in order to automate functionality that would normally be delegated to the command line. That doesn't apply here.

Fortunately, a few tools have arisen in the JavaScript world that embrace the Node.js and JavaScript ecosystem to provide massive amounts of functionality in tight little automated packages. By far the most popular are `grunt` and `gulp`, both of which have plugins that tie directly into `vulcanize` as a library.

Gulp

Gulp became popular after Grunt and addresses some of the drawbacks of the earlier tool. Most notably, it alleviates the verbose and heavy configuration syntax with pure code and the long wait times with a lot of asynchronous, stream-based beauty.

Gulp's community has exploded, and a lot of the major tasks that people use Grunt for have Gulp equivalents. The process of using this tool is excellent, straightforward, and scalable.

Whatever you choose, you will be taken care of; the drawbacks of one are benefits of the other. We'll be working with Grunt from this point on because it is the most popular tool at the moment and shows all signs of continuing to improve and grow.

Grunt

Grunt became popular nearly immediately after it came on the scene because it answered a question so many frontend developers were starting to have at the exact same time: "How do I manage these scripts I run every time I am at the end of development?" The road up to Grunt was littered with numerous options that linted your code, optimized it, built its modules, transpiled whatever, and then bundled everything up at the end. All of this quickly became unmaintainable, and *something* had to be done. Ben Alman, then at Bocoup, was looking for a way to automate the cumbersome maintenance tasks that came with managing many jQuery plugins, and out of that frustration came Grunt.

Grunt has its rough edges, but it was at the forefront of the modular, composable command pipeline, and as such, it amassed well over 1,500 plugins in short order, doing everything from simple concatenation to building AMD modules to transpiling EcmaScript 6 code to IE8-compatible JavaScript.

Grunt is not the answer to everything, but it's a great answer to the problem we have now: how do we automate the usage of Vulcanize to create multiple web component artifacts?

To get started with Grunt, it's important to know how it's architected. Grunt leverages Liftoff (*https://github.com/tkellen/node-liftoff*) (by Tyler Kellen and born out of the experience developing Grunt), which is a library that allows tools to look for local modules to bootstrap into its further functionality. That translates to Grunt being a global tool, grunt, that leverages local modules for the entirety of its functionality. The global grunt executable is installed via the grunt-cli npm package:

```
$ npm install -g grunt-cli
```

Whenever this executable is run it will look for a local installation of the grunt module. The reason it does this is to support various versions of the grunt *library* via any arbitrary version of the grunt *command-line interface*. With this pattern, you'll rarely ever need to update grunt-cli on any local box since the updated versions will be taken care of on a project-by-project basis. It's a clever style that has worked out well and is emulated by several projects now.

Running grunt without a local Grunt install will net you the following message:

```
$ grunt
grunt-cli: The grunt command line interface. (v0.1.11)

Fatal error: Unable to find local grunt.

If you're seeing this message, either a Gruntfile wasn't found or grunt
hasn't been installed locally to your project. For more information about
installing and configuring grunt, please see the Getting Started guide:
```

http://gruntjs.com/getting-started

In an established project, this almost always means that you have yet to run npm install. In a new project, it just means you haven't installed grunt locally yet (or, if you have already run npm install, then it means you haven't saved grunt as a development dependency to the project).

To get started using Grunt for our project, we need to initialize the project with npm so that dependencies can be tracked automatically, similar to how this was done with Bower in the previous chapter:

```
$ npm init
This utility will walk you through creating a package.json file.
It only covers the most common items, and tries to guess sane defaults.

See `npm help json` for definitive documentation on these fields
and exactly what they do.

Use `npm install <pkg> --save` afterwards to install a package and
save it as a dependency in the package.json file.

Press ^C at any time to quit.
name: *(x-dialog-grunt-vulcanize) x-dialog*
version: (0.0.0)
[ ...snipped... ]
```

npm walks through some basic questions in order to set some sensible defaults in our *package.json* file. This *package.json* file is npm's way of tracking the metadata associated with a project that either is published to npm or uses npm in some way. Even if publishing to npm is not in the pipeline (which it's not, until the developers explicitly support client-side modules), it's important to treat the metadata as important and relevant because it's used informally by other projects as a central metadata touchpoint for JavaScript-related projects. This includes accessing things like version data, test commands, author names, etc.

Installing Grunt plugins is trivially easy thanks to npm, and plugins are searchable from the official Grunt website (*http://gruntjs.com/plugins*). Many popular and well-supported tasks are simply named grunt-*<task>*. For example, Vulcanize's task is grunt-vulcanize, and it can be installed with npm alongside Grunt itself:

```
$ npm install grunt grunt-vulcanize
```

There was an initiative by Tyler Kellen shortly before Grunt 0.4 was released to centralize a wide number of common or first-class Grunt plugins under the umbrella of a *Grunt Contrib* team. Those who were part of the team were committed to keeping a large number of highly depended upon tasks (the grunt-contrib plugins) as up-to-date as possible with the most current Grunt version. Unless you know what you are doing, if there is a grunt-contrib-* version of the task you are looking for, it is recommended to start with that and only move on if it doesn't suit your needs.

Ben Alman created Grunt, but a lot of its functionality and consistency is largely due to Tyler Kellen and the Grunt Contrib team, which includes members like Sindre Sorhus, Kyle Young, and Vlad Filippov.

Gruntfiles

The basic configuration for Grunt build chains is done via a *Gruntfile* (spiritual kin to the *Makefile*, *Rakefile*, *Jakefile*, *Gulpfile*, and *build.xml*).

Running grunt with a local installation but without an available *Gruntfile.js*, you'll see the following error:

```
$ grunt
A valid Gruntfile could not be found. Please see the getting started guide for
more information on how to configure grunt: http://gruntjs.com/getting-started
Fatal error: Unable to find Gruntfile.
```

The *Gruntfile* is a plain old Node.js module that exports a function taking one argument, the context for the current project's installed Grunt version. That grunt object is used to load plugins, configure tasks, and set up build chains. A basic, albeit useless, *Gruntfile* looks like this:

```
module.exports = function (grunt) {

};
```

Running grunt now will net you the error:

```
$ grunt
Warning: Task "default" not found. Use --force to continue.

Aborted due to warnings.
```

One of the frustrating aspects of getting started with Grunt is the number of ways you can be tripped up without knowing why, or where to turn. Knowing the basic errors and their solutions will allow you to jump the hurdles a little bit faster and get productive sooner.

Grunt Tasks

Grunt runs on the concept of "tasks." Each task can lead to a JavaScript function or can be made up of an array of other tasks, forming a task chain that in turn can lead to functions or further task chains. Grunt doesn't have a single task built in, so by default it looks for a task registered as the `default` and complains if it cannot find one.

If we wanted to, we could define a very basic function that runs as the `default` task:

```
module.exports = function (grunt) {

    grunt.registerTask('default', function () {
        console.log('Running our own task!');
    })

};
```

Now we have a fully qualified Grunt installation that actually does something!

```
$ grunt
Running "default" task
Running our own task!

Done, without errors.
```

The text around our printed string is interesting and further clarifies what kind of framework Grunt provides. Chunks of functionality are broken up into "tasks" and can end with success or failure. Any task that causes errors in part of a chain will abort the rest of the execution and cause the process to exit with a failure. If we were to throw an error there:

```
module.exports = function (grunt) {

    grunt.registerTask('default', function () {
        throw new Error("I broke.");
    })

};
```

Grunt would respond appropriately, giving a warning and aborting with an error code:

```
$ grunt
Running "default" task
Warning: I broke. Use --force to continue.

Aborted due to warnings.
```

Admittedly, this `default` task is not very useful, and truth be told, we don't really want to be writing our own plugins at this time—that's not why one would choose Grunt off the bat. The real benefit comes in the community plugins.

Registering Tasks

In order for Grunt to be aware of a plugin installed via npm, you need to explicitly load it via loadNpmTasks. For example, to load our previously installed grunt-vulcanize plugin, we'd simply run grunt.loadNpmTasks('grunt-vulcanize');.

Many plugins register tasks themselves, but you'll either need to run grunt --help to find out what the exact names are or read the documentation. There is no standard mapping from plugin name to task name. The rule of thumb, though, is that the registered task is the most obvious possible name for the task. For example, for a plugin like grunt-vulcanize the task is assumed to be (and is) vulcanize, for a plugin like grunt-contrib-jasmine the task is assumed to be jasmine, etc.

Use grunt --help in order to get a lot of contextual assistance as well as a list of the registered tasks in a project.

We can run our vulcanize task with the command grunt vulcanize, but since that is the main focus of our Grunt configuration right now, it may as well be the default:

```
module.exports = function (grunt) {

    grunt.loadNpmTasks('grunt-vulcanize');

    grunt.registerTask('default', [ 'vulcanize' ]);

};
```

Running grunt now will net us a new error, indicating that there are no "targets" found:

```
$ grunt
>> No "vulcanize" targets found.
Warning: Task "vulcanize" failed. Use --force to continue.

Aborted due to warnings.
```

There are two major task concepts in Grunt: regular tasks, which are simple functions run without any explicit configuration, and "multitasks," which operate over a set of "targets." Targets are individually configured runs of a task, configured manually or programmatically in the Grunt config setup.

Grunt Configuration

The largest number of lines your *Gruntfile* will have will almost always be in the configuration block, an object passed into the initConfig method. For people getting started with Grunt, it always starts innocently, but once the grunt Kool-Aid kicks in and plugins start falling from the sky it quickly stretches to 50, then 100, then 300 lines long. There are ways to manage it, but that's for another book.

A Grunt configuration loading the `vulcanize` plugin starts off like this:

```
module.exports = function (grunt) {

    grunt.loadNpmTasks('grunt-vulcanize');

    var config = {};

    grunt.initConfig(config);

    grunt.registerTask('default', [ 'vulcanize' ]);

};
```

Task configurations are located in configuration properties of the same name. For a task like `vulcanize`, the configuration is located in a `vulcanize` property:

```
module.exports = function (grunt) {

    grunt.loadNpmTasks('grunt-vulcanize');

    var config = {
      vulcanize: {}
    };

    grunt.initConfig(config);

    grunt.registerTask('default', [ 'vulcanize' ]);

};
```

Multitask "targets" can be seen as conceptually equivalent to individual configurations of a task at one property deeper than the main task configuration. For example, for a target named "main" the task configuration would start at `config.vulcanize.main`, and to add another literal target, you'd add another key.

This is where the "library-first" pattern of tool development starts exhibiting true benefits. With `grunt-vulcanize`, we're not interacting with a command line at all; we're tying directly into the library itself, passing commands in and massaging return values into things that make sense to Grunt. This allows our previous work on the command line to translate over trivially, as the command-line options map to library options. Our primary `vulcanize` run then looks like this:

```
var config = {
  vulcanize: {
    main: {
      src: "components/src/x-dialog.html",
```

```
          dest: "x-dialog.html",
          options: {
            inline: true,
            excludes : {
                imports: [
                    "polymer"
                ],
                scripts: [
                    "jquery",
                    "jenga"
                ]
            }
          }
        }
      }
    }
};
```

Using that configuration, we can now use Grunt to automate our base vulcanize run:

```
$ grunt
Running "vulcanize:main" (vulcanize) task
OK

Done, without errors.
```

Now to add our CSP build, we just add a new target with similar configuration and one new option. You may be thinking that sounds like a *lot* of duplicated configuration if this pattern holds true for other tasks. Thankfully, Grunt has a way of setting common configuration through an options property at the root task configuration level. With no actual configuration except two targets and shared options, the properties of the vulcanize task then look like this:

```
var config = {
  vulcanize: {
    options: {},
    main: {},
    csp: {}
  }
};
```

Adding the configuration, we then have two distinct targets with the same sources and nearly the same options, except the CSP target has a different destination and one added flag:

```
var config = {
    vulcanize: {
        options: {
            inline: true,
            excludes : {
                imports: [
                    "polymer"
                ],
```

```
                scripts: [
                    "jquery",
                    "jenga"
                ]
            }
        },
        main: {
            src: "components/src/x-dialog.html",
            dest: "x-dialog.html"
        },
        csp: {
            src: "components/src/x-dialog.html",
            dest: "x-dialog-csp.html",
            options: {
                csp: true
            }
        }
    }
};
```

This is already a hefty amount of configuration for a seemingly basic task, and this is one of the primary complaints Grunt detractors have. I can empathize, but there's very little superfluous configuration there, so it's mostly a matter of recognizing where that configuration lies. With Grunt, it's passed in via one object to one method. With other tools, it's managed at different levels, but it still has to exist somewhere.

 For those actually following along in code, you'll notice that vulcan ize (and grunt-vulcanize) doesn't perform much optimization outside of the inlining and concatenation of scripts. The JavaScript file that is created isn't minified at all and can have a substantial weight to it. Ours, right now, already weighs in at ~30 KB. When gzipped, as it would likely be served from a server, it's 6.3 KB—which isn't much, but any extra weight shouldn't be tolerated. Minified, that code would be around 9 KB, gzipped and minified 2.9 KB —substantial enough savings to worry about.

Fortunately, we're using Grunt and can tie a virtually infinite number of plugins into our flow!

The method of chaining together disparate tasks may take some creativity, but the overall benefit should be obvious. To minify our JavaScript we'll use grunt-contrib-uglify, and we'll vulcanize the CSP build first in order to get all of our JavaScript in one place without excess configuration. We'll minify that file in place, and then run vulcanize on the CSP build to inline the minified JavaScript into a single HTML file. The total *Gruntfile.js* follows—see if you can spot the changes and the reasoning behind them (and don't forget to install grunt-contrib-uglify via npm install --save-dev grunt-contrib-uglify!):

```
module.exports = function (grunt) {

    grunt.loadNpmTasks('grunt-vulcanize');
    grunt.loadNpmTasks('grunt-contrib-uglify');

    var config = {
        uglify: {
            csp: {
                files: {
                    'x-dialog-csp.js': ['x-dialog-csp.js']
                }
            }
        },
        vulcanize: {
            options: {
                inline: true,
                excludes : {
                    imports: [
                        "polymer"
                    ],
                    scripts: [
                        "jquery",
                        "jenga"
                    ]
                }
            },
            main: {
                src: "x-dialog-csp.html",
                dest: "x-dialog.html"
            },
            csp: {
                src: "components/src/x-dialog.html",
                dest: "x-dialog-csp.html",
                options: {
                    csp: true
                }
            }
        }
    };


    grunt.initConfig(config);

    grunt.registerTask('default', [
        'vulcanize:csp',
        'uglify:csp',
        'vulcanize:main'
    ]);
```

Publishing with Bower

Up until this point, Bower has been used to manage the installation of dependencies. Now that the component is nearing completion, it's time to think about how consumers of this project might use it. Fortunately, if you've been managing dependencies with Bower already, then it becomes trivially easy to publish the package to the Bower registry.

The `x-dialog` package has already been using a *bower.json* file to keep track of its dependencies, so half of our metadata is already taken care of. Filling out the rest is fairly straightforward. Here's what it might look like:

```
{
  "name": "x-dialog",
  "version": "0.0.0",
  "authors": [
    "Your Name <email@email.com>"
  ],
  "description": "a dialog box web component",
  "main": "./x-dialog.html",
  "keywords": [
    "dialog"
  ],
  "license": "MIT",
  "homepage": "http://github.com/YOURUSER/x-dialog.html",
  "ignore": [
    "**/.*",
    "node_modules",
    "bower_components",
    "vendor",
    "test",
    "tests"
  ],
  "dependencies": {
    "polymer": "~0.3.3",
    "jquery": "~2.1.1",
    "jenga": "*"
  }
}
```

Proper Git tags are an important aspect of using Git repository endpoints for Bower packages. If a consumer specifies a version of a library—say, 1.2.1—the only way Bower can look for that in a Git repository is by looking up the tag name `v1.2.1`. An extremely important note is that the Git tag will always win. If `v1.2.1` is checked out and the *bower.json* file is specifying the package version is `1.0.1`, it won't matter;

whatever state the code was in when the repo was tagged `v1.2.1` is what will be installed.

The Wonder of the Web

This is yet another reason why Bower's usefulness is primarily due to the diligence of the web community, and another example of "worse is better." A vast majority of projects are actually managed in public Git repositories, and maintainers of public projects try to do a really good job of limiting backward compatibility concerns because they just have to.

The limitations of the Web have encouraged a substantial community of people to adopt standards that "just work." There have been *countless* attempts at making things "better," but they always fail when confronted with "what just works" because "what just works" gets adopted first.

In order to make the tagging easier and to ensure things stay in line, you can tag your Git repository and update the metadata with Bower itself. Issuing a `bower version 0.0.1` command will update *bower.json* and tag our Git repository with `v0.0.1` so that all we have to do from this point onward is push our changes live:

```
$ bower version 0.0.1
$ git tag
v0.0.1
$ git push --tags
```

Registering the Component

The metadata is in order and the code is working and packaged; it's time to make it public. Doing so is trivially easy with Bower and GitHub, because all we need to do is pick a name and link it to our public Git location. That's as easy as:

```
$ bower register x-dialog git://github.com/WebComponentsBook/x-dialog.git
```

Bower will indeed make sure this endpoint exists, but it won't do much more than that. Managing releases from this point onward is as simple as tagging our Git repository when we push new versions public. It's simple enough to be dangerous, so it encourages proper Git workflows and ensures a stable master branch.

To use our new component, install it like anything else:

```
$ bower install x-dialog
```

All of the dependencies will be pulled in and it'll be ready to go!

Summary

In this chapter we've solidified our process to account for packaging and deployment of our web component. After this point you should be able to create, test, package, deploy, and install an individual web component.

Some readers may feel compelled to question the value of all this if they never plan to distribute a web component publicly. The benefit of this process *is the process*. It is overhead that ensures appropriate dependency management, encapsulated logic, faster unit test suites, proper versioning of components, and overall easier maintenance *long term*. Getting into this flow may be a burden in the short term, but it pays off in spades.

CHAPTER 18

Final Words

Jarrod Overson

Congratulations—you know just enough about web components to start having a good time developing web applications. Once you start scratching the surface you'll discover a vast world that will delight and surprise you. Web components aren't the solution to every problem, though, and they present more questions than they answer —new questions that require new paradigms and patterns.

The field is also moving extremely quickly. To put it in perspective, when we started working on this book we planned to include a chapter on decorators, but that was eventually scrapped as the spec fizzled into nonexistence; the specs around creating custom components changed; Polymer went from alpha to beta to nearing a 1.0 release; and Chrome 36 stable shipped with full web component support out of the box. In a very short time web components went from a barely usable pipe dream to something that is legitimate and out in the wild.

This book is early for the realm of web components. We're on top of it all and intend this book to be a transitional primer for people moving from the existing world of widget writing to the new world of web component authoring. Hopefully you'll see multiple revisions of this book, each focusing on current best practices as the landscape evolves.

Where Do We Go from Here?

It is important to stay up to speed with the state of web components on the Web. This book is not able to be the final answer (yet…), so you'll need to seek out information and read the news as it occurs. We are already starting to see alternatives to the web components game; Polymer is actively changing before its 1.0 release; and Microsoft is approaching web components with force.

This section outlines some of the ones to watch, as well as a few hot sources of information to get you started.

Polymer

Polymer (*https://www.polymer-project.org*) has rapidly evolved from being an interesting project to being at the absolute forefront of custom element creation. It provides a slew of custom components ready to be used, and examples to help you get into them. When Google announced its material design (*http://bit.ly/dwc-google-md*) at I/O 2014, Polymer elements implementing the design were announced the same day, with tutorials at the conference. It is clear that Polymer is going to continue being a force and should be followed, respected, and questioned like any front-runner in a new technology. Polymer 0.8 incorporates some serious changes that will improve performance dramatically and shows that the team is dedicated to making Polymer the first choice in serious web component development.

Mozilla X-Tag

Mozilla's foray into the space, X-Tag (*http://x-tags.org*), is less opinionated than Polymer and attempts to ease the creation of custom components. The developers initially implemented their own polyfills, including an attempt at substantial shadow DOM shimming, but the group of early adopters eventually came to the conclusion that, to speed up adoption, standardizing on one set of polyfills was important. Now the polyfill implementations are the same as Polymer's, omitting the bulk of *platform.js* and including some extensions that provide support where Polymer lacks.

Mozilla (*http://brick.mozilla.io*) also showcases a large number of custom compontents built using X-Tag and is a great resource for seeing what you can do outside of the world of Polymer.

Polymer and X-Tag have had the freedom to run for years in controlled environments, though, and the assumptions they made a few years ago may no longer be the best of the breed when it comes to modern practice. Don't get me wrong, they very certainly do a lot of things very well, but the rest of the world is starting to jump on board and all the flaws that are revealed and changes that are made are going to spawn different implementations. Don't wait to find out who wins. Web components provide value *now*. Polymer is a fantastic solution, and the people putting it to use are doing beautiful things with it. It's attracting the best of the brightest and will surely be supported for many years in the future. If your environment doesn't need all of what Polymer provides, look around at the other options, but be realistic about your future support requirements; Polymer and web components may be a more viable option than you expect. Make sure the browsers you support are still highly used on *BrowserUsage.org* (*http://browserusage.org*) before omitting this valuable technology to accommodate potentially dying browsers.

document-register-element

Andrea Giammarchi created a polyfill for custom components (*http://bit.ly/dwc-cc-polyfill*) after some frustration with the heavy implementation promoted by Polymer. This version clocks in at around 2 KB and certainly works for basic implementations of custom elements. It isn't mentioned here because of its astounding uniqueness, but as an example of web components turning the corner into real-world usage.

WebComponents.org

Zeno Rocha, Rob Dodson, Addy Osmani, Eric Bidelman, and a slew of others have banded together to centralize modern information regarding web components on WebComponents.org (*http://webcomponents.org*). This is intended to be a reliable location for charting up-to-date practices and specifications and is a welcome addition. Web components have been a hot topic for over two years now, and this has resulted in a large number of out-of-date blog posts, repositories, and tweets floating around in the ether. Having a reliable, current website curated by some of the best in the field is a big benefit.

CustomElements.io

CustomElements.io (*http://customelements.io*) has been around for much longer than you'd probably expect and houses a wide range of community implementations of custom components. Since the site has been around for so long, it also contains references to a fair number of unmaintained components that may or may not run on modern versions of their dependencies. It remains, though, one of the top non-

Polymer and non–X-Tag resources for community component listings and will likely grow to become much more relevant as community components start becoming more popular.

Having a site dedicated to components is and will continue to be important. Applications and development flows that take full advantage of the HTML APIs presented by web components are going to benefit from staying in that environment. There's nothing preventing a developer from using a widget developed with this or that library, but it's that cognitive switch that will be optimized against. The future holds a large number of reimplementations of existing widgets in its path, and sites like Custom-Elements.io are going to be important to manage them.

Good Luck!

You're about to embark on a journey that this book's authors are going on with you. This is an excellent opportunity to make your mark on a virgin canvas. If you've ever been interested in reinventing your career, the modern Web holds unlimited potential for you right now.

Web components is a technology that will benefit from new minds and new ways of thinking about applications. You can easily become an expert in a field where expertise is highly sought after by expending some effort playing with cool technology. This, coupled with the fact that the technology will breathe new life into all existing widget ideas, means that there is a tremendous opportunity to become well versed in the technology simply by reimplementing old ideas in new ways.

Good luck, and we'll see you at the next revision!

Index

A

absolute positioning, 27
aligning elements, 61
Angular, 3, 190
Ant, 168, 209
API design, 12-14
APIs
    defining, 74
    dialog API, 124
    dialog custom element, 137
    in overlay construction, 57
    JavaScript, 163-164
    native, 47
    Polymer custom elements, 161-163
    query selector, 11
    resizeable, 83
    stubbing out, 39
    wrapper API, 105
artifact, 207
Asynchronous Module Definition (AMD), 16
attachedCallback, 132
attributeChangeCallback, 133
automated builds, 208

B

Backbone, 190
base class, 18-20
Bidelman, Eric, 102
block elements, 24
Bower, 169-172, 219
box model, 23-24
box sizing, 24
Browserify, 169
build, 207

build process, 207
builds, automated, 208

C

cleanup (see destroy function)
cloning nodes, 51-56
    cloneNode method, 52-53
    deep clone, 52
    definition and usage, 51
    and duplicate IDs, 53
    jQuery.clone, 53-55
code, importing (see importing code)
command-line interface, 205
component testing (see testing)
consumer, 207
content projection
    via content selectors, 118-119
    via content tag, 117
    distributed nodes and insertion points, 119
createdCallback, 132
cross-origin resource sharing, 145
CSS
    dialog, 95
    with imports, 142
    in Polymer, 155-156
CSS overlay, 64
custom elements, 4, 127-138
    defining properties and methods, 130
    dialog custom element, 135
    extending, 129
    in imports, 145-146
    and life cycle issues, 131-133
    naming conventions, 129
    registering, 128

resolving, 131
styling, 133-134
use of templates and shadow DOM with, 134
CustomElements.io, 225

D

deep clone, 52
default rendering layer, 34
default stacking orders, 34-36
dependencies, 15
destroy function, 63, 88
detachedCallback, 132
dialog class, 20
dialog CSS and HTML, 21
dialog custom element, 135-138
    in imports, 146
dialog template, 104
dialog template updating, 122-125
    dialog API, 124
    dialog markup, 123
    dialog show method, 124
    instantiating a dialog component instance, 125
dialog template wrapper, 105-107
dialog widget
    adding overlay to, 68
    adding z-index manager to, 47
    cloning and, 55
    concatenating JavaScript, 96
    making draggable, 78
    making resizeable, 92
    styling, 95-96
direction-based descriptors, 82
distributable, 207
distributed nodes, 119
Document Object Model (DOM), 3
    (see also shadow DOM)
    abstraction layer, 11
Document Object Model (DOM) APIs, 47
document type, 24
document-register-element, 225
drag and drop interfaces, 51
drag handles, 75, 81, 84
    (see also resizing elements)
draggable elements, 71-80
    defining an API, 74
    destroying, 78
    dialog widget, 78

drag handle creation, 75
element movement, 75-78
mouse events, 71-73
    (see also mouse events)

E

elements
    aligning, 61
    block, 24
    floated, 35
    inline, 24
    obtaining dimensions, 29
    positioning (see positioning)
Ember, 3
encapsulation, 109, 112, 117
    (see also shadow DOM)
Evergreens, 152
extending elements
    custom elements, 129
    native elements, 130
Extensible Web Manifesto, 165

F

fixed positioning, 28
flashes of unstyled content (FOUCs), 134
floated elements, 35
fundamental layout concepts, 23

G

Grunt, 168, 210-218
    configuration, 214-218
    grunt preprocess plugin, 16
    Gruntfiles, 212
    tasks, 213-214
Gulp, 168, 209

H

HTML imports, 3
HTML templates, 3
HTML5
    defining, 5

I

importing code, 139-147
    accessing content, 140-144
    accessing templates, 143
    applying styles, 142-143
    cross-domain considerations, 145

declaring an import, 139
and dialog custom element, 146
executing JavaScript, 144
loading custom elements, 145-146
parsing imports, 144
referencing documents, 141
subimports, 145
Inheritance pattern, 14
inline elements, 24
insertion points, shadow, 120-122
instance methods, 162

J

JavaScript
concatenating, 96
in imports, 144
in Polymer, 163-164
MVC libraries, 4
Node.js, 204
overlays, 65-66
PhantomJS 1, 190
PhantomJS 2, 191
prototypal inheritance, 14
jQuery, 151, 182-187
effects of removing, 183-186
features, 183
jQuery.clone, 53-55
query selector API, 11
value of, 186
for z-index manager plugin, 45
JXcore, 168

K

Karma, 191-196

L

life cycle issues, 12-14, 131-133
life cycle methods, 163
Liftoff, 210
listeners, 62

M

marketing impact and infuences, 190
mocha, 196-197
Model-View-Controller (MVC) libraries, 4
module loaders, 5
mouse events, 71-73, 81
best practices, 72, 82

and element movement, 75
mousedown, 72
mousemove, 71
mouseup, 72
resizing and, 85-88
Mozilla X-Tag, 224
MVC libraries, 4

N

naked attributes, 161
naming conventions, 129, 155
native elements, extending, 130
native templates, 102
Node.js, 168, 204
normal flow, 23-24
npm, 169, 211

O

offset parent, 25-26
optimization, 16
orphaned nodes, 16
overlay construction, 57-69
adding to dialog widget, 68
CSS overlay, 64
defining an API, 57
destroy function, 63
JavaScript overlay, 65-66
listeners, 62
positioning, 61, 62-68
(see also positioning)
scrollbars, 59-60
updating options, 62
utilities, 59-62
overlays, primary functions, 57

P

packaging and publishing, 203-221
automated builds, 208
Bower, 219-220
Grunt, 210-218
(see also Grunt)
Gulp, 209
terms and definitions, 207
Vulcanize, 204-209
parsing, 144
PhantomJS 1, 190
PhantomJS 2, 191
plugins, 45-47

Polymer
    adding style, 156
    block repitition, 159
    bound scopes, 160
    comparing to jQuery, 182
    conditional blocks, 160
    created versus ready, 164
    custom element API, 161-163
    data binding, 159
    delayed work, 164
    elements, 154-159
    events, 164
    external resources, 157
    filtering expressions, 157-159
    future outlook for, 224
    instance methods, 162
    JavaScript API, 163-164
    life cycle methods, 163
    multiple template directives at once, 161
    naked attributes, 161
    overview, 149, 151-154
    porting dialog to, 167-187
        (see also porting to Polymer)
    published properties, 162
    shims, 151-152
    template syntax, 159-161
    versions, 153
porting to Polymer, 167-187
    direct port, 169-182
    installing dependencies with Bower,
        171-173
    and jQuery, 182-187
    managing dependencies, 169-170
    reasons for, 168-169
position-based descriptors, 82
positioning, 24-31
    absolute, 27
    calculating, 29-31
    CSS overlay, 64
    dialog widget, 31
    dimensions and coordinates, 61
    fixed, 28, 62
    JavaScript overlay, 65-66
    offset parent, 25-26
    overlays, 62-68
    relative, 26
    relative to the document, 30-31
    relative to the viewport, 29
premature optimization, 16

Progressive Web, 168
projection (see content projection)
prototypal inheritance, 14
publish, 207
published properties, 162
publishing (see packaging and publishing)

R
rake, 209
registering custom elements, 128
relative positioning, 26
rendering layers, 34-36
resizing elements, 81-94
    API creation, 83
    binding event handlers, 85-88
    completed library, 88-92
    defining drag handles, 84
    destroy function, 88
    direction-based versus position-based
        descriptors, 82
    mouse events, 81
Rhino, 168

S
scrollbars, 59-60
Selenium WebDriver, 191
shadow DOM, 4, 109-125
    content projection, 117-120
    custom elements and, 134
    defining, 109
    events and, 122
    shadow host, 110
    shadow insertion points, 120-122
    shadow root, 110-111
    shadow root insertion points, 120
    style encapsulation, 112
    styling shadow root elements from parent
        page, 115-116
    styling the host element, 113-115
    trees, 120
    updating dialog template, 122-125
        (see also dialog template updating)
    using a template with, 111
shims, 151-152
single-page application (SPA), 142
Sizzle, 151
SPDY, 155
stacking contexts, 36-37
    creating, 42

determining, 39-41
    finding, 41
stacking orders, 34-36
static elements, 24

T

templates, 101-107
    adding to the DOM, 104
    content rendering deferment, 103
    creating and using, 103-104
    custom elements and, 134
    detecting browser support, 103
    dialog template, 104-107
    hiding content from the DOM, 103
    import, 143
    importance of, 102
    native, 102
    native browser templates, 101
    placing in markup, 103
    in Polymer, 159-161
    resource processing deferment, 102
    with shadow DOM, 111
testing, 189-201
    Karma, 191-196
    PhantomJS 1, 190
    PhantomJS 2, 191
    Selenium WebDriver, 191
    test specs, 196-199
tooltips, 62
type extension custom element, 130

U

Unixy, 209

V

Vulcanize, 204-209

W

W3C's Content Security Policy (CSP) recom-
    mendation, 208
Waldron, Rick, 186
web components
    beyond JavaScript, 17
    defining, 2, 5
WebComponents.org, 225
Webpack, 169
widgets, 11
    about, 9
    dialog, 31, 47
    life cycle, 12-14
    reasons for building, 49

Z

z-index, 33-48
    defining, 33
    managing, 37
        (see also z-index manager)
    overriding default stacking order, 35
    rendering layers and stacking order, 34-36
    stacking context determination, 39-41
    stacking contexts, 36-37
z-index manager, 38-45
    adding to dialog widget, 47
    API stub, 39
    converting to a jQuery plugin, 45-47
    examples, 44
    finding stacking contexts, 41
    modifying an element's z-index, 42-44
    utilities, 39-41

About the Authors

Jarrod Overson has been developing on the Web for over 15 years in both startups and global companies, and currently works at Shape Security. He founded Gossamer to help bootstrap companies into developing for the modern Web and has provided free community training on everything from Node.js to Backbone. Jarrod is an active proponent of and contributor to open source software, the creator of Plato, and a member of the Grunt, Marionette, and ES-Analysis teams.

Jason Strimpel is a Staff Software Engineer on the Platform team at WalmartLabs who specializes in the UI layer. Jason has been building web applications for the past 12 years. Approximately three years ago, Jason began specializing in the frontend, in particular JavaScript. Since then, he has worked with several component libraries and frameworks. However, he found limitations to these libraries when presented with uniquely challenging UI requirements, so he began developing his own custom components and catalog of helpers. He is an extremely passionate developer with a very bad sense of humor who loves simplifying the complexities that arise when building rich UIs.

Colophon

The animals on the cover of *Developing Web Components* are horse mackerel (*Trachurus trachurus*), also called *scad*. A species of jack mackerel in the family Carangidae, this fish is found primarily in the northeastern Atlantic and in the Mediterranean Sea.

The horse mackerel matures rapidly during the first few years of life and grows more slowly thereafter, commonly reaching between 15 and 40 centimeters in length. It has a metallic grayish-blue body with green tints, anchored by a large head and a forked tail. The fish's distinguishing marks include a black blotch on the edge of its gill covers. Its strong fins make it a fast, powerful swimmer; its common name derives from a legend that smaller fish could ride on its back like a horse.

The horse mackerel's diet mainly consists of small fish, crustaceans, and squid. Young horse mackerel have been known to shelter underneath large jellyfish, as they are immune to their venomous sting. These juveniles enjoy the dual benefit of evading predators—such as large tuna and dolphins—and garnering food remains from the jelly's prey.

Many of the animals on O'Reilly covers are endangered; all of them are important to the world. To learn more about how you can help, go to *animals.oreilly.com*.

The cover image is from *Wood's Animate Creation*. The cover fonts are URW Typewriter and Guardian Sans. The text font is Adobe Minion Pro; the heading font is Adobe Myriad Condensed; and the code font is Dalton Maag's Ubuntu Mono.

Get even more for your money.

Join the O'Reilly Community, and register the O'Reilly books you own. It's free, and you'll get:

- $4.99 ebook upgrade offer
- 40% upgrade offer on O'Reilly print books
- Membership discounts on books and events
- Free lifetime updates to ebooks and videos
- Multiple ebook formats, DRM FREE
- Participation in the O'Reilly community
- Newsletters
- Account management
- 100% Satisfaction Guarantee

Signing up is easy:

1. Go to: oreilly.com/go/register
2. Create an O'Reilly login.
3. Provide your address.
4. Register your books.

Note: English-language books only

To order books online:
oreilly.com/store

For questions about products or an order:
orders@oreilly.com

To sign up to get topic-specific email announcements and/or news about upcoming books, conferences, special offers, and new technologies:
elists@oreilly.com

For technical questions about book content:
booktech@oreilly.com

To submit new book proposals to our editors:
proposals@oreilly.com

O'Reilly books are available in multiple DRM-free ebook formats. For more information:
oreilly.com/ebooks

O'REILLY®

Lightning Source UK Ltd.
Milton Keynes UK
UKOW04f1630121016

285118UK00006B/13/P